101
Ways To Go Boating
for Under
$1000

101

Ways to Go Boating

for Under

$1000

Zack Taylor

BOATS EDITOR
Sports Afield MAGAZINE

Funk & Wagnalls • *New York*

Dedication

There was this gruff elegant man whose eyes when he smiled betrayed his gentleness and affection. He'd return from fishing expeditions and summon a small wide-eyed boy to peer at fat and silvery weakfish. His racing catboat would be ordered to the yard for repairs and he'd turn to the boy and tell him he better go along to show the Captain the way. And one day when the boy was seven years old the elegant man looked at him long and said, "Nobody will be using the duckboat this year. I'll have the hired man put it overboard for you."

Thus came my boat. I'd sail the duckboat downwind, then laboriously tow it back. I hadn't figured out how to tack yet. Besides it was scary away from shore. Years later the elegant man snorted at the idea that instructions in the ways of a duckboat would have been helpful. "That little boat was its own teacher. It would teach you what was wrong and right. And I could trust it to bring you home safe for supper."

So then, this book is dedicated to that elegant man, indeed all such elegant men, wise enough and brave enough to let loose a trustworthy little ship among small boys and girls. For if they are lucky a love will kindle. The boats will become beaten and scarred by years of willing service. And the boys and girls—like the elegant men—will never grow too old or too rich or too stuffy to eagerly set sail and harvest the endless varieties of pleasure little boats afford.

Contents

Introduction

This is a book primarily about small boats. You have to ask yourself why. Why small boats? Wouldn't everybody really prefer a big boat over a small boat every time? If they could afford it?

Answering that question in the affirmative tags you as a fair student of human nature. At the same time it reveals a woeful ignorance of what messing around in boats is all about. If you are setting out to buy the biggest boat you can afford—don't. The project is doomed to fail. After the initial excitement wears away, your boat is likely to join the ranks of the hundreds of thousands that sit empty and unused weekend after weekend. It will be one more silent, expensive proof that somebody's dream went bust. Like maybe yours.

What you've got to realize is that boats aren't objects

in themselves, not successful boats. They are vehicles that do something; take you fishing or cruising, let you sail, sightsee, waterski, paddle across Canada, explore, soak up sun, join a yacht club, win a race. It is a long list (which is why there are so many successful boats). In each case a specific objective is being achieved.

This gets to the point. There are dozens and dozens of watery objectives *only* small specialized boats can achieve. Countless different pleasures, some singular and immensely satisfying, they alone can deliver. No other vehicle can do what they do as well.

So this is a book first about these singular and satisfying pleasures. Only secondly is it a comparative accounting of small boats.

The fact that these little boats just happen also to be inexpensive is merely a coincidence.

But ain't it grand?

Canoe—World's Best Boat

In 1535, the French explorer Jacques Cartier came upon a boat that must have made him recoil in amazement. Before his eyes was a vessel the likes of which no white man had seen before.

It was paper thin yet unbelievably strong. Unlike the rowed craft he knew, it was paddled by a man looking ahead who could thus thread his way through tricky rapids or shallows. The long graceful shape enabled the craft to be carried easily over the many portages that interconnected the north country. He saw this boat and hundreds akin to it in use on all waters including the open seas and in sizes capable of transporting a single man or a ton of cargo. Most amazing of all, Cartier's exploration had penetrated the Stone Age. The Indian peoples he met possessed only wood,

1

bone, or stone tools. Yet these graceful craft, exquisite in form and function, were produced in quantity by them. The thought was chilling. How far back in antiquity did this craft go? How long had Indians been building them? The question was answered with a shrug and the simple response, "As long as there had been Indians."

The craft Cartier marveled at was, of course, the birchbark canoe. While other barks than birch were used, the range of so-called paper birch, in a belt from Atlantic-to-Pacific with its southern limits a line from Long Island to Washington state, made it the boat of the north woods. Elsewhere Cartier was transported in dugout canoes hollowed from giant logs. These too extend back in the dim history of man for they also can be, and are today, built with no tools other than fire and rocks. Here's how:

A giant tree is selected. A fire is built at its base. As the fire burns, the charred wood is pounded away with rocks. When the tree falls, the other end is burned away and fires shape both ends. A groove along the top of the now-prone trunk is insulated with mud and a fire started in the trough. As it burns, rocks are pounded steadily to work away the charred interior. Days, maybe months later, a hollow shell, blunt at both ends, emerges as a crude but serviceable canoe.

While today even in Africa or New Guinea dugout canoes would probably be chopped or adzed away with metal tools, the number of canoes in use around the globe must number in the millions. As you read this, canoes are carrying goods up the canals of Thailand, through the African surf, along the rivers of South America, China and India. No coastline of the globe is immune to the sight of one, crudely sailed or powered, transporting crowds of natives, their pets and domestic animals and wares.

To any traveler it is an observable fact that this ancient craft remains the world's best boat. Maybe not Lake Minnetonka's best boat, certainly not the best boat for Puget Sound or Lake Texoma, but it is a fact today if you travel to the watery ends of the earth, the craft that will take you will be a canoe. It may masquerade under a hundred aliases—sampan, pirogue, kayak, gondola, bateau. Variations on its basic cigar shape will be endless. Every material from skin and bone to shellacked paper will be employed to build it. But all are canoes. The ages have wreaked havoc and change upon the earth and the tools of man. This one has defied time. It is the immutable boat.

Traces of this awesome mystique still influence canoes and those who use and admire them. Whole libraries exist solely to chronicle its prowess. An entire National Forest and Park (Quetico-Superior) is reserved for its use alone by this country and Canada. (Even airplanes are forbidden to violate the sanctity of some parts of the Park.) Dozens of states maintain hundreds of miles of canoe routes along their lakes and streams and describe every inch of them in free booklets that make you long to set sail.

The oldest boating organization in this country is the American Canoe Association founded in 1880. It has never been more vigorous in its attempts to lure you into its fold, where for $6 you will be welcomed by pleasant people sharing a common interest.

Whether money is the root of all evil is problematical but money is most certainly the root of all canoe enthusiasm. Here is an accounting of what you can expect a fully equipped canoe to cost:

Equipment	Cost	Expected Life	Annual Cost
15-foot aluminum canoe	$239.00	20 years	$11.95
1.5 h.p. outboard motor	140.00	10 years	14.00
45 sq. foot nylon sail and needed equipment	168.00	10 years	16.80
Total...	$557.00	Total cost per year...	$42.75

You can carry your boat and all its accouterments anywhere in and on your car with no more special gear than a rope to lash the boat to the top, sitting on the life preservers. It can be raced under sail or in flat water and white water races sanctioned by a variety of canoe associations all over the nation, and the world. Your little ship will move easily and inexpensively under sail, oars, paddles or outboard and will carry two adults with ease.

You can use the boat for camping, pleasure paddling, sailing-racing, fishing or hunting by merely including or excluding the requisite items. If you have a large family, seventeen, eighteen and twenty-foot canoes will afford identical opportunities and the cost for the larger boat, motor and sail will still stay well within the $1000 limit. If at any time you lose interest, an ad in your local newspaper will reveal many anxious to purchase your boat after you take a fair depreciation.

If you can beat those statistics, if you know of some other kind of vessel that returns more boat for the money, please keep it a secret no longer. The world has been waiting over ten thousand years to hear of one.

There is something else. There is an additional element to canoeing, the places a canoe will take you, and the manner in which it will draw you along its path. You move slowly and you see all. You are close to the water and the wild. You are very recognizably man in nature. Yet, carried away by this kind of poetry and wallowing in their tradition, canoe enthusiasts tend to go overboard. They view canoes in general as the perfect boat and vigorously resist change. This is absurd. As sailboats, canoes are today hopelessly outclassed by many of the sailboats described elsewhere. The sensational advance of the modern outboard has left the canoe far in its wake. Small aluminum boats can utilize the high horsepower of the outboard; canoes cannot.

While some canoes are more unstable than others, all are vulnerable to treacherous and unexpected capsizes under certain conditions. To many, the possibility of tipping over in a canoe is a nagging and constant fear. A Maine guide calmly poling down a rapids appears indifferent to this danger, but you may rest assured it is never far from his mind.

Canoes do best the job for which they were intended. They are the ideal boat that can be paddled hour after hour by crewmen looking ahead. And they are very nearly the only boat that you can hoist on your shoulders and carry long distances without undue strain. Only the inflatables share this property with canoes and the balloon-like shape of the inflatables would dog your steps through many an overgrown portage.

To these basic attributes must be added a more genial virtue—versatility. One little sailboat shares with a canoe this characteristic which allows it to be sailed, paddled, rowed, or outboard powered, but in an age of specialization canoes remain refreshingly all-purpose. Mount the motor today and fish, paddle a wilderness stream tomorrow, sail the next day.

All these the canoe will deliver. If you figure the difference between what the canoe will cost you versus what you can sell it for and compute this on a yearly basis, an astonishing figure will emerge. Having fun with this boat will probably cost you about as much as the rubber wearing off the tires of your car. Even expensive canoes are delightfully cheap.

Hey! I bet that has something to do with why they've been around so long.

Choosing the Right Canoe

Canoe building became an art in Old Town, Maine, about 1880, and the company that still bears that name today offers without question the greatest collection of wood and fiberglass canoes. The GRUMMAN COMPANY came into its own after World War II when it turned its vast experience building aluminum flying boats to building aluminum canoes. Today GRUMMAN's sales dominate the canoe business.

Both these excellent companies offer free catalogues that picture the canoes and many accessories you will find discussed in the pages ahead and listed in the catalogue section. I would suggest you send for both. (Any dealer can also furnish them.) By singling out these companies I don't mean to suggest that other canoes listed are not just as good—or better. It is simply that being aware of the variety available and fine points of each will equip you to be a better buyer. You will be less susceptible to some salesman who may, or may not, know what he's talking about.

Studying canoe catalogues in front of a fire on a long winter night is strong medicine. What it will do besides unravel your cares is make you think about your boat's ultimate use. Are you going into partnership with this canoe to fish? Or sail? Or power with an outboard? Or float rivers near your home, or far away? Maybe you want to do all those things with your boat. Okay, but will you be alone, or will your wife and kids want to come along too? By gosh, the plot is thickening already and we haven't even begun to worry about what material the creature should be made of. "Which should I buy— a wood, fiberglass or aluminum canoe?" is usually the first question people ask me. But they shouldn't. First comes that very personal, albeit haphazard and subject to change, decision of basically what do you want to do with this here machine. No one can help you with that. It's between you and Neptune.

Basic Canoe Facts

The Double-Ender

Bascially this a boat for paddling or sailing. Within a given size, two things determine its performance—beam and bottom shape. If the beam is narrow, the boat will generally be faster but load carrying ability will be penalized. The roundness of the bottom also has a great effect on performance. If the curve where the side meets the bottom (the chine) is abrupt and the bottom is basically flat, the canoe will be less tippy. It will carry more load, but it will be slow and clumsy. If the curve is sweet, like a champagne glass, your boat will be fast and sporty, but at a cost—the cost of stability. A racing canoe or kayak is so tippy you hardly dare sit on the seats. You paddle them from kneeling or sitting positions with your weight directly on the bottom. But the pencil shape enables them to fly through the water with little resistance.

As you shop around, look for the differences in bottom shapes. Some boats will be slim, sleek and rounded. They'll be "hot," that is fast and tippy. A fatter canoe with a flatter bottom won't be quite so fast but it will be more stable, less likely to flip you. More important, if you plan to cruise, or carry a few pals along, it can handle much greater loads. Whether anyone likes it or not, the GRUMMAN seventeen-foot standard canoe is probably the one single model in widest use throughout the world. Possibly some earlier wood models may have been more popular, but since aluminum came into acceptance more of this one model have been made than any other. Because of its wide acceptance among real canoe pros, its compromise shape can well be used as a guide.

Square-Stern Canoes

Although the double-ender will always remain the choice of the long-distance paddler, the square-stern canoe has widespread use. When light, high-horsepower outboard motors came into use, those who used canoes on big water turned to them to move their boats quickly over the long distances. Squaring the stern made handling the motor much safer and easier, and it was found at low paddling speeds that the lack of flowing underwater lines aft did not detract from paddling performance over short distances. With the motor removed, the canoe can be portaged as easily as any and, although white water ability is somewhat reduced, the square-stern boat is equal to the double-ended version facing waves in a storm.

The square-stern is your boat if you plan to motor long distances under power or to use the canoe as you would fishing big lakes where the motor would seldom be off the stern.

What Size?

The great nineteenth-century outdoorsman, Nessmuk, claimed ten pounds of cedar ought to carry one hundred pounds of man. His personal canoe, hit upon after years of trial and error, was ten and a half feet long, carried a twenty-six-inch beam and weighed an incredible twenty-two pounds. This he claimed was good for a single man weighing from one hundred forty to one hundred seventy pounds. For a two hundred-pounder he advised adding six inches to her length, two inches to beam.

Two companies today, that I know of, build eleven-footers. As the specifications will show, both have considerably more beam than Nessmuk's and weigh twice as much! Despite the uneasy feeling that the old master knew more about the subject than I do, I would suggest a boat in this size today only if back-packing were very nearly the most important consideration; for example, if the canoe were to be used to fish remote lakes that could only be reached by hiking. Otherwise I would go to a thirteen-footer which will handle two people without gear at the cost of only a few pounds extra weight. Two people in the eleven-footer would be marginal.

At the other end of the scale, are the OLD TOWN and GRUMMAN twenty-footers, and some even larger canoes built mostly in the northern United States or Canada. You have to take these boats as you find them. You see a boat you like, inquire who the builder is, and ferret him out. It may be more of a job than you expected. Quality varies, but locally built boats I've seen reflect pride of workmanship. OLD TOWN builds a twenty-five-foot canvas and wood canoe but it is more a boat for boys' camps than anything and doesn't reflect in size and power its long length.

Generally speaking, if you plan to head into the wild blue yonder with two people and their duffle, go to a seventeen-footer. With three people or more, step up to eighteen to twenty feet. One man can portage a twenty-footer weighing one hundred twenty pounds and with two men it is a breeze. The extra size is usually worth the paddling handicap, especially if a motor is used or you plan your cruise to utilize currents. In small lakes or local floats the fifteen to sixteen-foot size is adequate.

Capacity

The GRUMMAN BOAT COMPANY lists the following capacities for their standard canoes with six-inch freeboard amidship. Weights in pounds.

Double-enders	Square-sterns
13-foot— 750	15-foot—1028
15-foot— 890	17-foot—1100
17-foot—1050	19-foot—1550
18-foot—1146	
20-foot—1600	

Outboard Power

You have two choices for powering a double-ended canoe: with a bracket that fits all the way aft over the stern, or on a side bracket next to the aft seat. Both will push the canoe at the same speed. The side mount is far more comfortable. Your hand lies naturally on the steering arm as you face forward, and the motor can be lifted on and off and refueled with some ease. The disadvantages are that the canoe doesn't turn as readily and that it is possible, if the canoe gets sideways for the underwater housing, to hit an obstruction and flip the boat over. Also, should you gun the motor toward the boat, it tips the hull, and if your weight happens to be thrown just the wrong way at the wrong time the boat can capsize.

Steering with the motor aft requires you to hold one arm nearly behind you while your neck is craning around to see ahead. (This is also a problem in smaller square-stern canoes where you cannot sit sideways.) If you have a feel for Rube Goldberg inventions, an extension steering handle can be rigged that alleviates much of the suffering. The aft mount puts the motor out of the way when tipped up and steering is more positive. Some companies offer a wishbone stern mount. In this the underwater lines are the same as in a conventional model but the stern, instead of being sharp, is spread slightly to accommodate the grips of a small motor, a satisfactory —even nifty—arrangement.

Speed and Fuel Consumption

At my request, the KIEKHAEFFER CORPORATION ran tests at their Lake X proving ground. While the tests were made with their Mercury 4 h.p. and 6 h.p. outboards, speeds and fuel consumption of other motors in the same horsepower range would be comparable.

Mercury 4 h.p. on 17-foot GRUMMAN *with 1000-pound load*

Miles per hour Speeds	Miles per gallon
2	10½
3	12⅔
4	14½

Miles per hour Speeds	Miles per gallon
5	16¼
6	15⅞
7	14

(This indicates the most efficient speed to run is between 5 and 6 m.p.h. With the canoe loaded level this would be approximately when a discernable bow wave started to form.)

Mercury 6 h.p. on 18-foot GRUMMAN *with 1000-pound load*

Miles per hour Speeds	Miles per gallon
2	9½
3	11½
4	12½
5	12⅞
6	12¼

(Between 4 and 5 m.p.h. is the efficient speed for this larger boat and motor.)

What Size Motor?

The charts show the relatively slow speeds attainable with as large a motor as a standard double-ender will absorb. Only in larger sized square-sterns, where the stern is flat enough to "plane" or lift the boat some, can you expect more. There are a lot of good 1.5 h.p. outboards on the market that rate high with canoe buffs because they are so light (twenty pounds). They don't have much push, however. Speeds might average 4 m.p.h. tops with a thirteen-footer, 3.5 m.p.h. with a fifteen-footer and less than 3 m.p.h. with a seventeen-footer. They lack the soup to push against strong winds or currents.

Portaging

The long cigar shape of a canoe makes it surprisingly easy to carry—*once* you get it on your shoulders and *if* you have a comfortable yoke. Only if you have to climb uphill or manage the boat in a high wind does life suddenly seem not worth living. If you're all tiger, one hundred pounds or more is no hardship because of the gracefulness of the load, kind of like its being easier to carry two buckets of water than one. If you anticipate much carrying or some particularly mean carries, GRUMMAN offers lightweight models out of .032-inch aluminum versus the .051-inch sheeting of their standard models. Weights are shown in the listings but don't expect the lightweights to stand the gaff as well or even last as long.

Keel or No Keel

A keel helps keep the boat gliding on course between paddle strokes. But this effect makes it harder to turn the boat quickly as you would do maneuvering down rapids. Canoes for lakes should have keels. Wilderness cruising canoes are better left keelless. A variation is offered in the GRUMMAN shoe (flat) keel or the bilge keels found on wood canoes. Either way the matter is not particularly critical. You'll find plenty of keeless canoes on lakes and one veteran wilderness canoeist I know of uses a keeled canoe because he found one for sale cheap. He says he can't tell the difference.

Wood, Aluminum or Fiberglass?

There are beautiful canoes all priced, weighing and shaped approximately the same, the only difference being the material each is made of. Which is best? You'll hear much heated oratory about this subject; unfortunately those involved usually have an ax to grind and their words are suspect. The traditional nature of most canoe buffs causes them to cling desperately to the past. The best way to get a grip on the subject is with some facts. Fact 1: Thousands of wood-canvas canoes that have retained their beauty and serviceability over half a century are in action as you read this. Fact 2: Local canoe builders too small to have (or want) national distribution usually build in wood. This is being somewhat influenced by Fact 3: Since a canoe's curvy shape imparts great strength to fiberglass, and fiberglass—unlike aluminum—can so easily be curved, fiberglass builders are a small segment of the market but their numbers are growing faster than others. It is in this area that you will meet newer and more radical hull shapes. Some represent real design advancement.

Here are some more material facts. (See also the chapter on buying used for repair considerations in alumi-

num or fiberglass.) Wood and aluminum are hard to
repair; fiberglass is a cinch. Aluminum catches on rocks
in white water (waxing helps), wood is okay and fiberglass slips right off. Aluminum is noisy. Fiberglass and
wood are silent. Fiberglass needs waxing now and then
to keep looking nice. Aluminum takes care of itself unless you paint it—then you have to keep after the paint.

When all is said and done on this question, and it
never will be, my views are thus: Avoid a wood canoe
unless you can buy it at a sacrificial price and/or a local
builder is offering a style obtainable only in wood. The
choice between fiberglass or aluminum should be made
on the basis of shape, price, availability, etc.—that is, on
factors other than material. The differences between the
two materials these days are miniscule. This is especially
true now that real beauty is being built into fiberglass
canoes. Aluminum will never be an aesthetic material—
serviceable, yes; friendly, no.

Neo-Canoes

Both ALUMA CRAFT and GRUMMAN make a boat that
is like a square-stern canoe but the after end is broad-
ened so the vessel can handle slightly more outboard
power. They call them Sportboats. Since the overall
motor weight—not horsepower alone—is a determining
factor, these boats have profited by the continued lowering of weight-to-horsepower ratios. They will handle
today's 10 h.p. neatly and deliver flashy performance.

Speeds in excess of 20 m.p.h. can be expected and while the boat will be "hot" it will be safe enough in knowing hands. Weight and shape make the boat easy to portage and performance under paddles can still be considered fair. Vital statistics are shown in the listing.

Sail Canoes

The canoe that you are going to equip with a sail can be wood, aluminum or fiberglass, it doesn't make any difference. In fact, your canoe can even be a kayak. Many hotshot sailing models are kayaks. For simplicity's sake I'll refer only to canoes but most everything that follows applies equally to kayaks.

Length is one limiting factor. About thirteen feet is the minimum-size canoe that can be sailed well except by children. The bigger and beamier the better. If the bottom is rockered (curved) so much the better. If not, don't worry. A shallow water keel or no keel is better than a projecting keel. If your canoe does have a keel you might have to help it come about with the paddle. Or perhaps you can grind or plane the keel at the ends.

Either square or conventional stern is okay. The square stern (in effect) brings the rudder closer to the helmsman. Weight distribution is slightly more critical in a square stern. You must lift the stern slightly so it won't cause drag. A canoe should make almost no wake at all, even at high speeds. Here is the specialized sailing gear you'll need and the costs:

Mast Step and Thwart

This is a thwart, sometimes a seat, with a hole for the mast and a fitting that fastens to the bottom to receive the butt of the mast. About $10.

Leeboards

Or hydrofoils. Leeboards are offered by all well-known canoe manufacturers. They keep the canoe from skidding sideways. Hydrofoils also do this but add stability and sail-carrying power as well. Leeboards are simpler and cheaper. Good ones are varnished mahogany bolted to a cross frame which, in turn, bolts to the gunnel. You need two, since when the boat heels the windward board lifts out of the water. Store-bought cost: $40.

Rudder

You can steer a sail canoe with a paddle, but not make it perform with snap and crackle. Get a rudder. Some steer with ropes on conventional sterns. Some use long tillers. Cost: $30. Or make your own, side mounted.

Mast and Sail

Usually these come as a package. There are good commercial sails, and there are bad. Most are too small for the canoes they go on. Put a small baggy sail on a seventeen-foot canoe and it is like putting a 10 h.p. motor on a seventeen-foot outboard. It won't perform. Most canoe companies sell nylon sails. Although cheaper, nylon isn't as good a sail material as Dacron. Nylon stretches and loses its efficient airfoil shape under stress. All small racing sailboats use Dacron sails except for spinnakers.

The bigger your canoe the bigger sail it needs. In light winds you need a huge sail, in heavy winds a small one. Some sails can be shortened (reefed), most small boat sails can't. You hold the boat flat by luffing or hiking (leaning) out.

RIVERS AND GILMAN recommed a 50-foot lateen sail for their thirteen and fifteen-foot canoes. GRUMMAN recommends a 45-footer on their fifteen-foot canoe. RIVERS AND GILMAN recommends a 70-square footer on their seventeen and eighteen-foot boats. FOLBOT hoists a well cut 50-square-foot sail on their fourteen-and-a-half-foot kayak and a 60-footer on the seventeen and a half Super Folbot. Their sails are available in nylon and Dacron. OLD TOWN has long put two 55 or 65-square-foot sails on their seventeen to twenty-footers and when you hoist this much power aloft, the world starts moving past you a great deal faster. OLD TOWN now offers a good Dacron lateen sail and a new marconi-headed sail of racing caliber. GRUMMAN's sails are much improved but are not as yet racing quality.

Sail area is by no means the whole story. Efficiency is. There are three kinds of sail rigs. Since you'll meet them in other sections let's take a look at each.

The lateen rig hoists a two-spar V on its side up a short mast, thusly $<$. Almost all the sailing boards use it. It was invented by the Phoenicians two thousand years ago, if anybody cares. Modern design has made it no better, probably worse. The reason it is used is that the short mast keeps the center of effort low. This makes the boat less tippy.

The sliding gunter rig is a two-mast arrangement. The standing mast is used to hoist a sliding mast higher. It too keeps weight and effort low, and doesn't flatten the sail against the mast on one tack like the lateen. GRUMMAN offers this in Dacron with 65 square feet of area.

The most efficient rig is the marconi. FOLBOT offers a marconi canoe sail with a jib, 100 square feet in all. All the small sailers use this but as you can see they have twice as much beam as most canoes.

I am presently rigging a sail on a seventeen-and-a-half-foot SAWYER Cruiser canoe. It is an extremely light, sporty boat with fine ends and a thirty-three-inch beam. I think I'll go for a 40-square-foot sail so I can race it in the Cruiser class. On a standard seventeen-footer and bigger I would recommend the 75-square-foot lateen. On smaller canoes, go for 40 and 50-square-foot lateens.

The American Canoe Association has for years sanctioned canoe races all over the country. You will certainly want to consider their class requirements. A study of them also shows the varying degrees of "hotness." Keep in mind that sail area and horsepower are comparable. The more you have, the faster you go.

ACA SAIL CANOE CLASSES

	Inter-national	A	B	C	Cruising	Dixie
Length, max.	17	21	18½	18½	18	18½
Length, min.	16	18½	17	16	unlimited	16
Beam, min.	37½	36	34	33	5/32 of length	33
Rudder	yes		rudder or paddle		paddle	rudder or paddle
Max. sail area	107½	135	105	55	40	30
Mast height	no limit	20	18	16	13½	11
Number crew allowed	1	3	2	1 (min.)	1 (min.)	1

The very fastest canoes are those International class canoes. These are decked and special shaped hulls with centerboards. They can hold their own with anything that sails. ROYAL SAILBOATS, 1815 Northwest Blvd., Columbus, Ohio 43212, has kits.

Class A, B, C and Dixie must be stock canoes from any manufacturer, aluminum or wood. Cruising class can be fiberglass. Decks can be added but the middle third of the boat must remain open. Class C is the most popular.

Two sources are moving forward rapidly to popularize and modernize sailing canoe rigs. In the bargain they offer really helpful advice to the do-it-yourselfer. Here is material available from the American Canoe Association:

C—*101 Class "C" Sailing Canoe* NEVERSINK—55 sq. ft.
Outline drawing and sail plan suitable for wood,

canvas covered, fiberglass or aluminum stock hull—
for pleasure or racing. (free)

Development of the Crusing Canoe Sailing Rig—Brief
review of sail rig changes in the last 60 years—contains
design sketch of original sail plan, leeboard, etc. (free)

ACA Monograph No. 1—*Combined rig, Cruising Sailing
Cat & Class "C" Sloop*—Describes sail plan and construction.

ACA Monograph No. 2—*Learning to Sail a Canoe*—Elements of a sailing rig; how to adjust them for best
results.

ACA Monograph No. 3—*Construction of Masts*—How to
build a hollow wood, or aluminum tubular, mast with
luff rope slot.

The following include plans, drawings, and how-to
advice:

R—38   Detail of Boom & Mast Fixture—For hoisting
luff spar with marconi sail, as in C-101 sail design.

R—12   Design of Leeboard suitable for Class "C"
canoe.

R—15   Design of Leeboard Thwart for Cruising & Class
"C" Canoes.

R—20   Detail design of tubular aluminum mast for
Cruising and Class "C" Canoes—with luff rope
slot.

R—24   Detail design of hollow wood mast for Cruising
and Class "C" Canoes—with luff rope slot.

R—33   Simple aluminum tilting rudder.

R—33A Method of attaching aluminum rudder to canoe.
R—37   Simple rudder-tiller arrangement for open sail-
       ing canoes.

The first two items are free. The others are 10 cents
each. Copies may be obtained by writing:

> Roger Wilkinson, Sailing Editor
> *The American Canoeist*
> Oak Tree Lane
> Rumson, N. J. 07760

Another private individual has been working very
experimentally with canoe sailing rigs. He is Mr. Bruce
Clark of 115 McGavock Pike, Nashville, Tenn. He has
compiled his thoughts, building drawings, and helpful
advice in a six-page booklet, *Canoe and Kayak Sailing
Rigs, Leeboards and Hydrofoil Stabilizers,* which he sells
for $3.75. It is well worth the price if you get interested
in the sport.

In conjunction with the SAWYER CANOE CO., he has developed a radical modified lateen rig with one hundred
and seven square feet of sail and a peak twenty-two feet
long. Hydrofoil leeboards mounted on an eleven-foot-
beam "hiking board" make this a fast, innovative rig.
Final price for the sail kit is about $225; all details are
available through the company.

Other Canoe Racing

There are a number of sanctioned events for racing
under muscle power alone, sometimes in standard ca-

noes but usually in boats so specialized they can be used only for that purpose. Newest and fastest growing is white water slalom racing where one and two-man canoes and kayaks go up, down, across and occasionally under raging rapids through "gates" (poles hung from wires over the stream). The boats, all fiberglass, look like big bananas and have earned that nickname. They are fully decked over and the crew is sealed in watertight by skirts attached to round cockpits. A feature of these races is the eskimo roll. When the boats tip over, the paddler lunges and brings the boat upright, a la Nanook of the North. Men, women and boys participate in the sport, which originated in Europe and has only recently become popular here. I covered a big slalom race in Vermont a couple of years ago and the high point was when a youngster, maybe ten years old, came bouncing eagerly down the path next to the river obviously following a contestant and shouted, "Come on, Mom!"

Flat water racing has been a fixture of the land for many years, mostly in the midwest, and the so-called C-1 canoe, shaped like a spear, is raced in Olympic competition. Again the American Canoe Association is the guardian of it all. As you can see, their literature is the place to pursue both these subjects further, for he-men (and he-women) only, but fun. Races and various events in commercial canoes should be pursued through the divisional branches of the ACA.

Canoe Literature and Organizations

Despite a long and most rewarding acquaintance with the subject I am continually surprised at the immense body of literature devoted to canoes and their use. It is probable that no suitable inch of canoeable waterway anywhere in the world has not been traveled and written about. Not only are these accounts available, they have been catalogued in a bibliography, a fact as astounding as anything about these remarkable boats. The book is *Bibliography of Canoeing* by Arthur Bodin. It lists all books, magazine articles, pamphlets, poems, movies, short stories, etc., on canoes that have been published in the United States from 1700 (!) to 1954. This bibliography should be available at most big-city libraries. Obtaining the articles referred to will probably require more effort. If the local librarian cannot offer help in locating desired material, you may request a copy of it via the Library of Congress, Washington, D.C. 20013. Even whole books out of copyright can be copied at a reasonable cost (around $10) on microfilm or Xerox sheets.

Canoe Organizations

Trying to list all the canoe organizations is as ambitious as the attempt to list all the printed material. However, the most obvious is the American Canoe Association numbering some 1100 members. All correspondence should be directed to Miss Doris Cousins, Secretary, 400 Eastern Avenue, New Haven, Conn. 06510. Membership costs $6.00 annually, which includes a subscription to the quarterly, *The American Canoeist*. The American Canoe Association is affiliated with the International Canoe Association composed of clubs of most European countries and the Canadian Canoe Association (% Mr. Frank Clement, 3210 St. Joseph Blvd., Lachine, Quebec). European canoe and kayak interest is much higher than in this country, and club memberships there will number in the tens of thousands. Do you know why? Because Europeans don't have lots of money, and gasoline costs are high; inexpensive boating is a must for them.

The American Whitewater Club joins together the various slalom-racing groups and publishes a quarterly, *American White Water*. Address: Robert Hawley, 1925 Hopkins St., Berkley, Cal. 94707.

The United States Canoe Association is an aggressive new organization that is designed to break out of the traditional and conservative mold of the canoeist. Address Charles Moore, 6338 Hoover Rd., Indianapolis, Ind. 46260.

In addition to the large organizations there are a number of local canoe-kayak associations found all over the country. The way to locate these is through inquiry to various local divisions of the ACA, as most will be affiliated. The divisions and the addresses to gain further regional information are as follows:

ATLANTIC DIVISION
Anthony A. Szatkowski
422 Sheffield Rd.
Ridgewood, N. J. 07450

CENTRAL DIVISION
Raymond J. Axelson
329 S. Midler Ave.
Syracuse, N. Y. 13206

DIXIE DIVISION
James F. Kearney
Rt. 1, Box 418
Orange Park, Fla. 32073

EASTERN DIVISION
Lucian E. Levesque
Rt. 6-A
Columbia, Conn. 06237

MIDDLE STATES DIVISION
James T. Raleigh
7207 Churchill Rd.
McLean, Va. 22101

NORTHERN DIVISION
Aubrey E. Ireland, Sr.
100 Adelaide St. W.
Toronto, Ontario, Canada

NORTH WEST DIVISION
Dr. Theodore Houk
6019 51st Ave. NE
Seattle, Wash. 98115

PACIFIC DIVISION
Clyde Leaming
11914 Oxnard St.
North Hollywood, Cal. 91606

ROCKY MOUNTAIN DIVISION
Dannie Makris
630 W. 3rd St.
Salida, Colo. 81201

WESTERN DIVISION
not available

Canoe Trip Assistance

Traditional canoe states like Maine, New York, Wisconsin, Minnesota and the Canadian provinces of Ontario and Quebec have for many years offered comprehensive guides to their canoeable waterways. However, with the widespread adoption of boating regulations and registration, the various states have increased personnel and expanded assistance programs. A letter to the Division of Recreational Boating at the state capitol will almost certainly return information on your state's canoeable waters.

The American Canoe Association is another fine source for canoe trip material. Not only are the offerings inexpensive, they are also available, which is sometimes more important. They offer the following:

ACA Pamphlets

1. *Notes on Conducting a Youth Canoeing Regatta*
2. *Racing Paddling—Single Blade*
3. *Racing Paddling—Double Blade*
4. *Creating Junior Paddlers by Means of the War Canoe*
5. *Cruising in the South—How to Run a Cruise*
6. *Elements of Safety and Whitewater Paddling Technique*
7. *Increasing Your Skill in, and Enjoyment of, Whitewater Canoeing*
8. *The Lagoon Tilt, and Some Streamside Geometry*
9. *Regional Cruise Guide—New Jersey River Trips*
10. *Cruising the Delaware*
11. *Regional Guide—Potomac River*
12. *Cruising the Paw Paw Bends of the Potomac River*
13. *Cruising the Cacapon*
14. *Guide—Chicago Area River Trips*
15. *Design and Construction of a Fiberglass Whitewater Slalom Canoe*
16. *A New Build-It-Yourself Method of Making Kayaks and Canoes*
17. *How to Build a Canoe Sailing Rig*

45. *Leeboards for the Lazy Sailor and Ideas from a Danish Canoeist*
46. *Advanced Paddling Techniques—Slalom and White water II*
47. *War Canoe Training*
48. *Slalom Training and Strategy III*
49. *Slalom and Whitewater Rules* (25 cents)

Single copies of any of the above are 10 cents each, unless otherwise noted, and may be obtained from *The American Canoeist,* 1217 Spring Garden Street, Philadephia, Pa. 19123.

Books and Pamphlets of Various Publishers

*British Columbia Scenic Routes—*The British Columbia Travel Bureau, Victoria, British Columbia.

*Canoeing in Alberta—*Alberta Travel Bureau, Edmonton, Alberta.

*Interesting Saskatchewan Trips—*The Saskatchewan Tourist Building, Regina, Saskatchewan.

*With Canoe and Paddle in Manitoba—*Bureau of Travel and Publicity, Winnepeg, Manitoba.

*Ontario Lakes and Streams—*Department of Travel and Publicity, Parliament Building, Toronto, Ontario.

*Quebec Waterways—*Quebec Tourist Bureau, Quebec City, P.Q.

*Cruising in New Brunswick—*Government Bureau of Travel Information, Fredericton, New Brunswick.

Water Trails of Nova Scotia—Department of Publicity, Halifax, Nova Scotia.

Prince Edward Island Canoeing—The Prince Edward Island Tavel Bureau, Charlottetown, P.I.

Canoeing—The standard text on all phases of canoe training. Available from all local chapters of American Red Cross. (445 pages, photographs, and drawings) $1.25.

Basic Canoeing by American Red Cross. An excellent guide for the beginner. Available at all American Red Cross chapters. (63 pages) 40 cents.

Canoeing by W. VanB. Claussen. Merit Badge Handbook of Boy Scouts of America. Available from department stores selling Boy Scout equipment. (60 pages, illustrated) 35 cents.

Canoeing Manual—An excellent guide for teaching progressive canoeing skills. Includes thorough section on equipment and techniques, trips, weather, canoe camping, and teaching methods. Published by American Camping Association, Bradford Woods, Martinsville, Ind. 46151. (96 pages) $1.00 plus 20 cents postage.

Canoeing Whitewater—in Virginia, Northeastern West Virginia, and the Great Smokey Mountain area of North Carolina. By Randy Carter. Covers two thousand miles on sixty-six streams in four states. In addition, there is a large amount of general information with which the canoeist should be familiar. Randy Carter, 158 Winchester Street, Warrenton, Va. 22186. $5.00.

New England Canoeing Guide—A comprehensive guide to cruising every water east of the Hudson River. Appalachian Mountain Club, 5 Joy Street, Boston, Mass. 02108. (475 pages) $5.00.

Exploring the Little Rivers of New Jersey by James and Margaret Cawley. A charming and classic book describing the scenery and history associated with each river. Rutgers University Press, New Brunswick, N. J. 08903. (169 pages, photographs) Cloth $4.50, paper $1.95.

Canoeable Waterways of New York State by Lawrence I. Grinnell. A comprehensive review of all canoe cruising waters in New York and nearby areas. Pageant Press, 101 Fifth Avenue, New York, N. Y. 10003 (349 pages) $5.00.

Whitewater Sport by Peter D. Whitney. A comprehensive introduction to the exciting sport of running rivers and rapids in kayaks and canoes. Ronald Press, 15 E. 25th Street, New York, N. Y. 10010. (120 pages) $4.00.

A Whitewater Handbook for Canoe and Kayak by John Urban. Published by Appalachian Mountain Club of New York. Available from Louis J. Matacia, 7414 Leesburg Pike, Falls Church, Va. 22043. $1.50.

Blue Ridge Voyages (2 volumes) Volume 1:—A guide covering ten one- and two-day canoe trips in Maryland, Virginia and West Virginia. Includes equipment checklist, and local canoe clubs. (40 pages) $1.75. Volume 2: More one- and two-day trips in the same three states.

(40 pages) $2.00. Available from Louis J. Matacia, 7414 Leesburg Pike, Falls Church, Va. 22043.

Connecticut River Guide—The Appalachian Mountain Club, 5 Joy Street, Boston, Mass. 02108. $2.00.

Delaware River Recreation Maps—A 10-map folder covering the Delaware River from Hancock, N. Y. to Trenton, N. J. Available from the Delaware River Commission, 25 Scotch Road, Trenton, N. J. 08608. $1.00.

Canoeing on the Connecticut River—Showing upper Connecticut River, available free from Department of Resources and Economic Development, State of New Hampshire, Concord, N. H. 03301. (32 pages)

Vermont—Map showing canoe trails in the state. Available free from the Vermont Development Department, Montpelier, Vt. 05602.

Wilderness Crow Wing Canoe Trail—Map. Write to Vacation Information Center, Department of Business Development, State Capitol, St. Paul, Minn. 55101.

Alaska; Swan Lake Canoe Route—Map. Write to Bureau of Sport Fisheries & Wildlife, Room 409 Federal Building, P. O. Box 1287, Juneau, Alas. 99801.

Ohio Canoe Adventures—Pamphlet available free from Ohio Department of Natural Resources, 1500 Dublin Road, Columbus, Ohio 43212.

Maine Canoeing—Pamphlet with map describes twenty-seven Maine canoe trips. Available free from Department of Economic Development, State House, Augusta, Me. 04330.

Michigan Canoe Trails—Pamphlet available free from Michigan Dept. of Conservation, Lansing, Mich. 48924.

Colorado Canoeing Information—Available from State of Colorado, Department of Game, Fish & Parks, 6060 Broadway, Denver, Colo. 80216.

Canoe Trips in Florida—Write to Florida Development Commission, Tallahassee, Fla. 32304.

Adirondack Canoe Routes—Booklet available from the State of New York Conservation Department, Division of Conservation Education, Albany, N. Y. 12226. (30 pages plus map)

Iowa Canoe Trips—Booklet available free from State Conservation Commission, East 7th & Court, Des Moines, Ia. 50308.

Washington; 17 Whitewater Rivers—List and brief descriptions. Department of Commerce & Economic Development, General Administration Building, Olympia, Wash. 98501.

Canoe Runs in New Jersey—Brief description of fourteen rivers in New Jersey. Available free from State of New Jersey, Department of Conservation and Economic Development, Trenton, N. J. 08608.

Pawcatuck River & Wood River—Folder showing boat landings, portages, and campsites, map and description. Available free from State of Rhode Island, Department of Natural Resources, Veteran's Memorial Building, Providence, R. I. 02903.

Forests and Parks of Maryland—Map with description of camp grounds. State of Maryland, Department of Forests and Parks, State Office Bulding, Annapolis, Md. 21404.

Wisconsin Water Trails—A very fine booklet showing forty-eight canoe trips in excellent detail. Available free from the Wisconsin Conservation Department, Box 450, Madison, Wisc. 53703.

Canoe Trails—Fourteen maps of canoe trips in Indiana. State of Indiana, Department of Natural Resources, State Office Building, Indianapolis, Ind. 46209. (25 cents)

Camping and Boating in Delaware—Free brochure from Delaware State Development Department, Dover, Del. (Includes map)

Missouri Ozark Waterways—Available from Missouri Department of Conservation, Information Section, Box 180, Jefferson City, Mo. 65101. $1.00.

Idaho—Salmon River & North Fork Snake River—State of Idaho Fish & Game Department, 600 S. Walnut, P. O. Box 25, Boise, Ida. 83701.

Illinois—Illinois Canoeing Guide—Thorough description of twenty-three canoeable state rivers. Free from Illinois Department of Conservation, 102 State Office Building, Springfield, Ill. 62706.

Kayak Advice

Most people don't realize that the underwater lines of what used to be called an "express canoe" and the small kayaks are exactly the same. The difference is only in the freeboard (height of the side above water). Its freeboard can be much less because the kayak is decked over. The boats are usually so narrow and tippy that the occupant must sit directly on the bottom. Paddling is usually done with a two-bladed paddle. This is also an easier paddle with which to control the smaller canoes since their short length quickly strays off course using a single paddle. Kayaks are far more popular than canoes in Europe and most come from there.

The canoe is the great load carrier but the average kayak is fast and sporty and incapable of gracefully handling much more than the one or two occupants and a minimum of gear. With their slim lines they are good sailors but capable of utilizing only modest horsepower. Although there are some fine kayaks being imported into this country, as well as some hotshot build-it-yourself varieties, your choice of kayaks is limited compared with canoes. None are aluminum that I know of. The newer white-water models are all fiberglass and the imports incorporate folding capability and are usually canvas or rubber over collapsible wood frames.

The tiny kayak is without question the most seaworthy small vessel ever conceived. The eskimo's seal-skin-over-bone boat features complete water integrity, something the new *Queen Elizabeth* lacks. A wave can break right over the kayak with no harm to the vessel. The small flashy kayaks are the sports cars of the canoe world. I remember standing on the bank of Vermont's Black River and watching three young huskies in white-water helmets pouring it to their kayaks across a smooth stretch. They were throwing a six-inch bow wave and driving the boats nearly ten miles an hour with thrusts of the paddle that bent the limber ash with each stroke. Just at the bank, they wheeled their boats sideways, skidding to a stop just like a motorcycle hot rod, only it was water not dust that they showered into the air.

Canoes at a Glance

Here are the best known canoe and kayak manufacturers with particulars on their boats. Prices are list prices without local taxes or freight charges. Weights are as presented and variations in actual practice can be expected by pessimists. Double-ended unless otherwise specified.

GRUMMAN BOATS, GRUMMAN ALLIED INDUSTRIES, Marathon, N.Y. 13803

Model	Length	Beam	Weight	Cost
13-ft. Standard	13'1½"	35⅜	58	$235
13-ft. Lightweight	13'1½"	35⅜	44	249
15-ft. Standard	15½'	35⅛	69	239
15-ft. Lightweight	15½'	35⅛	55	255
17-ft. Standard	17¾'	36⅛	75	255
17-ft. Lightweight	17¾'	36⅛	60	269
18-ft. Standard	18¾'	36⅝	85	269
18-ft. Lightweight	18¾'	36⅝	67	285
20-ft. (Guide model)	20	40⅛	115	350
20-ft. (War canoe)	20	40⅛	117	389
15-ft. Square-stern Standard	15	36	77	269
17-ft. Square-stern	17	36⅝	85	285
19-ft. Square-stern	19½'	40⅛	116	369
Sportboat	15'3"	43	112	349

Custom colors—$40; custom shoe keels on 15, 17 and 18-foot standards only—$25; outboard bracket—$16.50; gunwale covers— $18; lateen sail rig (45 sq. ft. of nylon) complete with rudder, leeboards, etc.—$168; Gunter sail rig (65 sq. ft. of Dacron) complete—$198.

OLD TOWN CANOE CO., 58 Middle Street, Old Town, Me. 04468

Wood-canvas canoes

Model	Length	Beam	Weight	Cost
Lightweight Canoe	11'	3'	47	$315
Lightweight Canoe	13'	3'	53	335
Lightweight Canoe	15'	2'11"	58	355
Featherweight Canoe Wood/Dacron	15'	2'11"	46	375
Square-End Canoe	15'	3'4"	115	450
Guide's Special Canoe	16'	3'11"	70	375
Otca Canoe	16'	3'	70	375

Model	Length	Beam	Weight	Cost
Otca Canoe	17′	2′11″	75	395
Molitor Canoe	17′	2′11″	80	450
Guide's Special Canoe	18′	3′	85	415
Otca Canoe	18′	3′1″	80	415
Square-End Canoe	18′	3′6″	130	495
Guide's Special Canoe	20′	3′3″	100	475
War Canoe	25′	3′8″	180	985

Fiberglass canoes

14-ft.	14′	36	72	$275
16-ft.	16′	36½	82	305
18-ft.	18′	37	92	335

INDIAN BRAND (Rivers & Gilman Products) Hampden, Me. 04444

Fiberglass canoes

Papoose	11′	40¾	45	$145
Brave	13′	35	58	169
Squaw	15′	36	69	215
Princess	17′	35¾	80	235
Chief	18′	38	85	258
Penobscot Square	16'	38¼	99	299

HERTER'S, INC., Waseca, Minn. 56093 (Famous mail order house)

Fiberglass canoes

15-ft.	15′	35	95	$165
18-ft.	18′	35	102	184
17-ft. Square-stern	17′	36	105	180

HANS KLEPPER CORP., 35 Union Square West, New York, N.Y. 10003

Fiberglass canoes

SL-7 One-Man Kayak	13′6″	24	30	$244
Spider One-Man Kayak	15′	24	30	244

Model	Length	Beam	Weight	Cost
Tramp One-Man Kayak	15'	27	40	250
Bummler One-Man Kayak	15'	27	50	250
K-2 Two-Man Kayak	16'	28	70	320

ALUMA CRAFT BOAT DIVISION, Alpex Corp., 1515 Central Avenue N.E., Minneapolis, Minn. 55413

Aluminum canoes

Sport Canoe	14'2"	37	90	$299
C-15 Canoe	15'	37	67	229
CO-15 Canoe	15'	37	82	269
Quetico Canoe	17'	36	69	249
C-17 Canoe	17'	37	85	259
CO-17 Canoe	17'	37	92	289

(Sport canoe is similar to GRUMMAN Sportboat; CO-15, CO-17 have "Wishbone" transom to take small motors.)

CORE CRAFT (Bemidji Boat Co., Inc.) Bemidji, Minn. 56601

Fiberglass canoes

Model	Length	Beam	Weight	Cost
CR-16 Canoe	16'3"	35	65	$199
CS-16 Canoe	16'3"	35	70	259
CRS-16 Canoe square-stern	16'3"	35	68	259
CSS-16 Canoe square-stern	16'3"	35	73	259
C-17 Canoe	17'3"	36	80	269
CSS-17 Canoe square-stern	17'3"	36	105	289

FOLBOT CORP., Stark Industrial Park, P.O. Box 7097, Charleston, S.C. 29405

Champion Kayak Racer, FG	16'	2'1"	45	$210

Folding Kayaks

There are several firms importing kayaks from Europe whose principal feature is that they can be quickly knocked down and stored in a small package. Construction is canvas or strong synthetic rubberized material over a wood frame. Some models are square-stern and can take high outboard horsepower. These are by no means inconsiderable boats. They offer all the canoe advantages of power, sail and paddle options. In fact one of the boats listed below actually made a transatlantic crossing. The catalogues are free. That of FOLBOT is exhaustive in nature and many accessories listed therein would prove handy in any canoe.

AMERIMEX CORP., 122 West 30th St., New York, N.Y. 10001

Model	Length	Beam	Weight	Cost
Sprite Single-Seat Kayak	11'	2'4"	30	$198
Sprite Two-Seat Kayak	13'9"	2'5"	42	240
Adventurer Kayak	18'	3'	75	297
Adventurer 4-Seat Kayak	19'7"	3'6"	80	372

FOLBOT CORP., Stark Industrial Park, P.O. Box 7097, Charleston, S.C. 29405

Glider 2-Seat Kayak	14'6"	3'1"	58	$146
Sporty 1-Seat Kayak	15'	2'8"	54	189
Super Folbot				
3-Seat Kayak	17'6"	3'1"	74	225

KAYAK CORP. OF AMERICA INC., 7 East 38th St., New York, N.Y. 10016

Pioneer Models

Kayak 430 SL	14'3"	2'1"	43	$260
Kayak 450 S	14'8"	2'2"	46	250

Model	Length	Beam	Weight	Cost
Kayak 520 Z	17'	2'9"	59	325
Ketch 520 ZS (SA 68)	17'	2'9"	90	450
Kayak 540 G	18'	2'9"	68	355
Ketch 540 GS (SA 68)	18'	2'9"	100	480

Nautisport Models

Nautyak Jr. Kayak	13'9"	2'5"	46	$250
Wanderer Kayak	17'	3'	60	275

HANS KLEPPER CORP., 35 Union Sq. West, New York, N.Y. 10003

Tradewind Sloop	14'3"	4'4"	140	$1,098
Aerius One-Man Kayak	15'	2'4"	50	298
Aerius Two-Man Kayak	17'	3'	70	369

SAWYER CANOE CO., Oscoda, Mich. 48750

Fiberglass

Sport Canoe	15'9"	36"	57	$198
Cruiser Canoe	17'9"	33"	61	250
Guide Special Canoe, F	18'	36"	73	235
Safari Canoe				
square-stern	18'	36"	79	265
Super Canoe	18'6"	33"	59	250
Saber	24'	35"	70	350

(Very long, low freeboard, sporty canoes. Saber designed for Texas Water Safari 550-mile race.)

RAYMOND DODGE, 1625 Broadway, Niles, Mich. 49120

Model	Length	Beam	Weight	Cost
Rob Ray Kayak	17'	26"	33	$360
Slender Kayak	17'	20"	36	265
Zepher Kayak	17'	22"	33	335

(Imported from Denmark, Slender is fiberglass; the others, mahogany veneer. These are competition boats.)

The Little Aluminums

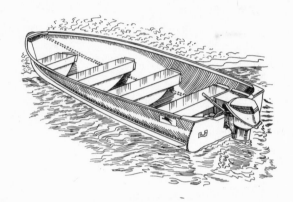

Every year since about 1950 far more boats have been built out of aluminum than any other kind of material. There are ten reasons why. It's cheap. Those are the first nine reasons. The other reason is insignificant.

Light, strong and incredibly rugged, sheet aluminum can be riveted with giant machines that slam out a boat almost with one blast. Clank. Bang. Screech. A new vessel is born. The aluminum in it costs $30. The machine to build it and the man (more often today a woman) to feed the monster costs $50. Freight adds another $15. A dealer grabs his $25. State and Uncle Sam's taxes take another $30. At the end there sits the boat in all her glory for $149.95, representing ten to twenty years of fun on the water. You and me along with hundreds of thousands of others vote yes.

Big vessels are built out of aluminum. Along the Gulf Coast most of the fast boats that speed oil rig crews out to the offshore platforms are aluminum. Several renowned builders offer express cruisers in the twenty-eight—sixty-foot range. And most of the firms that build the johnboats and cartoppers we will talk about have on the top of their lines aluminum runabouts and small cabin cruisers.

We are going to stick to the little fellows. Not just because they are inexpensive, but because they do their job so well for so long for so little. Somehow there has been a perfect marriage here. These rugged half pints apparently do what most of the people want them to do. Since marine aluminum alloys are nearly impervious to corrosion, the years will show only a slight oxidation on the skin. The shiny look disappears and if you need the exercise you can repolish it whenever the fancy strikes you. (Travel and house trailer supply houses have the best aluminum polishes. Met-All is a good one.) Aluminum can be etched with a chemical wash to roughen the surface after which it will take regular paint well. If you want to do the job yourself, roughen the surface with stainless steel wool or sand it with emery cloth. The trend today in our effluent (excuse me—affluent) society is to paint the little boats. Starcraft, which probably commands most of the cartopper market, does so because they feature a jazzy white hull with a cool green-blue interior. The boat looks sharp but, alas, when paint goes on it must be maintained thereafter.

At first glance it might seem we had placed severe limitations on our choice of boats with the $1000 maximum. But anyone who feels that way simply doesn't understand that boats must be measured only by how well they do the job for which they were intended. If you tow a travel trailer or live in really rugged (i.e., 4-wheel drive) country you must cartop. There isn't any other way to take a boat along. Maybe you want to launch off a beach. You have to have a light boat. If its bream or bass you want, plus the ability to race down a bayou to and from them, you can spend ten times $1000 but you won't get a boat that will do the job better than an outboard-powered johnboat . . . cost $800 if you insist on the best.

We are talking about real boats. You've seen plenty of bathtub boats around. Unsafe and breakable. These are phony boats with phony price tags. (If a "boat" costs $49.50 and splits the first time out, you've had an expensive boat ride.) Our vessels may be tiny but they must be worthy of their heritage. They must be long lasting, seaworthy, comfortable, capable of taking care of you even if things go wrong. They must be real boats, designed for a specific job, apologies to no one.

The little aluminums pass these tests with flying colors. At the bottom of the list you'll find eight-foot prams. This is about as small as a boat can get and still retain some boat characteristics. Below this size you have a watertight box at best. Most little boats this size are called prams and they have square ends like a johnboat. This gives them more room and, of course, weight carrying ability. Let's look at a typical pram:

HARWILL *8-foot flat-bottom aluminum pram.*   *Cost*
Weight is 56 pounds; beam, 42″
She'll carry 316 pounds .... $ 99.00
Two six foot oars. Two life cushions 16.00
Mighty Mite 1.7 h.p. outboard 94.50
                                              $209.50

Not only is this little bucket all boat. It and others like it are the *best* boats if you want one to slip in the back of a station wagon and fool around on a lake near you. The backs of most modern wagons have a span of about forty-four inches from side to side on the floor, maybe fifty-four inches window to window. A little pram like this slips in easily, rides on the tailgate like a duck and when you come home at night, jumps up on its storage rack like any well-trained boat should. Is there a reservoir near your home? There is near mine. It is crossed by two abutted roads and while boats are permitted, they aren't encouraged enough for the water company to put in any launch facilities. Sound familiar? It is a condition you see everywhere. What's more, the doggone reservoirs don't get much fishing pressure. Nobody is equipped to fish them. The other fishermen all have big expensive boats, not little fellows like my pram that will slip down the banks of those abutted roads as easy as pie. In minutes I'm in another world. No houses or other people. Just me and the fish and all this within view of the New York skyscrapers, if I climbed a tree. The pram makes it possible.

The other end of our $1000 restriction stops us at about sixteen feet. At that, you may have to resort to some judicious buying to get the *maximum* performance out of a boat and motor combination. By maximum, however, I mean just that. This will be a tremendously rugged, heavily framed vessel with husky freeboard and a top brand motor that will drive it in the 30-mile-plus speed range with your family aboard, including Rover. Make no mistake, we are talking now about a big water boat capable of handling most anything rivers, huge impoundments and bays or sounds can dish up. And if the boat can't handle it, it is capable of hauling you to safety fast.

It will be an open boat, however. Seats won't be the fancy back-to-back type that allegedly make up into bunks. (Ever try sleeping in one?) You'll find wood thwarts with flotation underneath, three in the twelve and fourteen-footers, probably four in the sixteen-foot-ers. There won't be any windshield to shelter you, no forward deck, no vinyl trim, no chrome. Runabouts with all these are okay, they have a purpose. A windshield is nice when you are blasting along at 30 m.p.h. all day. The forward steering station balances out the boat well. And it is comfortable to be able to stand up and walk around in the after cockpit. Nevertheless, you are prob-ably spending at least twice as much for the pleasure. (I'll describe later how to solve the open boat windshield and balance problems.)

In return for its luxury the runabout sacrifices some important options. Auxiliary power is out. You can install a special mount for a smaller engine but few do, and oars simply look too foolish with such high free-board. In a sixteen-foot open boat, oars and oarlocks are more natural—and can bring you home! A smaller motor goes easily on its transom. Cartop potential is denied the runabout, and its weight in the eight hundred—nine hundred-pound total weight class makes launching from minimal or nonexistent ramps unwise.

As the listings show, you can get open aluminums in the sixteen-foot range and the johnboats go up to twenty feet, mostly because they are used extensively by commercial fishermen on mid-west rivers. But the vast majority of the boats we're talking about are twelve to fourteen feet. These are the sizes that seem to work best. All the outboard people have aimed motors specifically at them and sweet machines they are. At the twelve-foot

end of the range weights are attractive for one-man cartopping, the boats perform wonderfully with one man
aboard and only slightly less wonderfully with two. The
fourteen-footers handle two persons easily, can still be
cartopped, are a dream to trail and. properly powered
go like blazes. I've had each of these rigs so let's take a
closer look.

	Cost
GRUMMAN *12-foot cartopper:* Weight 97 pounds; beam, 44"; capacity, 650 pounds	$230.00
Oars, three preserver cushions, portable running lights, Danforth anchor, 8-foot chain and 60-foot rode	45.00
9.5 Johnson outboard and remote tank	495.00
Trailex aluminum trailer, 4 ply tires	155.00
QUIK-N-EASY cartop racks with hold-down clamps and side roller bar	45.00
	$970.00

I've used this boat in the big open water sounds along
the Carolina banks and once slid easily down New York's
blustery, beautiful Lake Champlain in a howling north-
easter. Its performance never ceased to amaze me and
why they discontinued it is a mystery. With little boats
like this, weight is all-important. They depend on their
buoyancy to live through heavy seas. If allowed, they can
jump right over waves. Load them down with two and
three persons and they are dangerous and tippy. You've
robbed them of their natural defense. This is true with

a fourteen-footer as well. Only when you get into a husky sixteen-footer with high sides (freeboard) can you start carrying a lot of weight safely. With the 9.5 h.p. outboard my twelve-footer can top twenty m.p.h. I am able to cartop and trailer it easily alone. On long highway trips where I don't want the bother and expense of trailering, plus having to leave the boat outside a motel all night, I cartop it. Gear is locked inside the car. When fishing gets hot around home and I am using the boat most every day she lives on the trailer. I save myself the chore of hauling motor and equipment in and out. (See how being lazy broadens your experience?) Winters, the vessel hangs from the garage rafters.

I am intrigued by the rigs commonly used by the ocean-going cartoppers where I live. These hotshots launch through the surf and fish the open Atlantic. Walkie-talkie equipped, they never range more than a few miles from shore but on many a night you'll see them plugging home against a strong wind. You can't help but admire the little boats they use, capable of taking Neptune's rough stuff most of the time and instantly scooting up on the beach and hiding in a garage when they can't. The boats they use are all twelve or fourteen-footers. The sixteen-footers weigh too much to drag up and down the sand. Here are the facts on the boat I have on order.

STARCRAFT *Super Starfish:*   *Cost*
Length is 14′1″; weight, 185; beam, 57″;
capacity, 800 pounds .... $ 299.00

Oars, three preserver cushions, portable running lights, Danforth anchor, chain and rode	45.00
Mercury 20 h.p. and portable tank	510.00
Gator galvanized steel trailer, 4 ply tires	125.00
QUIK-N-EASY cartop rack with hold-down clamps and roller bar	45.00
	$1024.00

The lesson here is that the additional horsepower is the culprit that will push the cost up. You'll find with a sixteen-footer the same thing holds true. Here is a very rough scale of relative costs for boat and motor combinations that still retain good performance. You can go below these horsepowers if you have short distances to travel and efficient speeds are not important. But to plane the boat and get all the hull will deliver out of it, these minimums are barely adequate. Besides, who likes a slow boat for long? Prices are list prices for the *best* equipment.

12-foot hull $200	minimum h.p. 6	$325
	maximum h.p. 9½	$480
14-foot boat $300	minimum h.p. 9½	$480
	maximum h.p. 20	$510
	minimum h.p. 20 (2 persons)	$510
16-foot hull $400	adequate h.p. 33 (3 persons)	$600
	maximum h.p. 40	$690

I might elaborate at this point on the easy launching virtues of the aluminums. Usually you can launch a boat where the site is poor. Even if you are afraid to back the car down, most of the time you can unhitch the trailer and push it into position. Gravity is on your side. Getting out is a different story. The way I've done it dozens of times is to unload the boat, tie a line to the car and slowly drag the vessel to high ground. The boat is so light and metal so strong no harm is done to the boat aside from a scratch or two on the bottom.

Generally speaking these small boats can be separated into four classifications. Prams, johnboats, cartoppers and open utilities. The last two classifications get somewhat hazy when you consider that about two hundred pounds is all two men can lift to the top of a car without such mechanical aids as we'll discuss. A 20-h.p. outboard weighs about eighty pounds, horrible enough to lift. But motors in the 35-h.p. class are in the one hundred thirty pound area. Even if you could hoist it into your car's trunk, it would pick the front wheels off the ground; well, almost. We've made it tough on our price requirement by including a trailer even in the twelve-footers that cartop in a breeze. But there isn't any question in most cases you price yourself beyond the trailer option if you stretch much farther than fourteen feet. That's what makes the fourteen-footers the most popular and you'll notice a wider variety of hulls in this length than any other.

Just so nobody feels left out it must be added that a

very few johnboats and a couple of cartoppers are made out of fiberglass. There isn't anything wrong with them. It is just that fiberglass isn't *quite* as light and, when light, *quite* as strong as the metal. Hence, where these two qualities are all-important, aluminum gets the nod. That is not true, though, where prams are concerned. Most of these are built to be used as dingies for larger auxiliary sailboats. Since this is a boat area dominated by fiberglass, the dingies are almost always fiberglass. Often they are made to be rigged with small sails. To make a sailer out of a little teeny boat like this requires a complicated bottom shape, a series of curvy planes. You can mold fiberglass any way you want easily. It's strong when curvy, less so when flat. Aluminum is manufactured in flat sheets and the price tag stays low when aluminum boats are built with flat sections, which is why there are so few fiberglass johnboats. We'll arbitrarily rank these small sailors in the chapter with the vest-pocket sailors, which is where they shine. If you slip one in the back of your station wagon, however, and use it to break the smallmouth bass record, don't tell me I said it couldn't be done. I'll be too busy cheering to notice anyway. You'll see the few aluminum prams in the johnboat listings.

When you're shopping for any aluminum boat, it's important to know the thickness of the skin of the aluminum hull. More thickness (and frames) makes the boat stronger, longer-lived and heavier. It also costs more. Extremely lightweight boats will have skins as thin as

.032 inches, which you'll remember was the gauge of the GRUMMAN lightweight canoes. Most lightweight aluminum boats are, or ought to be, in the .050-inch range. Fifteen-footers should be around .060 and eighteen-foot boats should be .070 inch. When you learn that ocean-going crew boats have skins only a little more than twice .hat, .160 to .180 inch, you can see why small aluminum boats are so tough.

Aluminum in Salt Water

This is a question that is slowly being relegated to the oblivion it so richly deserves. Today any of several alloys that combine copper, magnesium, zinc and silicon with aluminum are impervious to salt water and weather. (Look at the way aluminum storm screens and windows stand up today.) The only way you can get in trouble is to couple another metal to the aluminum. Then an electric current is generated (the flow of which you can actually measure with precision instruments) and this will eat away the less resistant metal. For example, if you attach a brass bolt, the brass will disappear; if an iron bolt, the aluminum around the bolt will be corroded. Stainless steel doesn't work this way. It and aluminum are compatible and all the aluminum masts on those big auxiliaries we were just talking about are held together with aluminum extrusions and stainless fittings, both of which last for years.

The only other area of caution is the use of bottom

paint. The reason is the same. Copper bronze paint offers the traditional protection against barnacles, worms, grass fouling and the like, but it contains copper which will quickly pit the aluminum and eventually eat right through it. So too will mercuric compounds, another metallic poison barnacles and company don't like. This can be used on aluminum bottoms if a barrier coat of paint, usually zinc chromate, precedes it. The undercoat insulates against the electrical flow. All this became history, however, when a new substance, quite poisonous to marine growths and wholly compatible with aluminum, was discovered a few years ago. Bis-tributyl—tin oxide or TBTO for short—is now marketed by several companies, the latest of which is MERCURY OUTBOARDS. Use TBTO bottom paint, don't run any steel or brass or bronze fittings through your hull and you're safe.

Cartopping

Ever since I bought my first car I've been hauling boats around on top of them. The only exception was when I owned a car with a rumble seat, then I stuck a pram in the rumble seat. (I've still got the pram. I *wish* I still had the car—a 1934 Plymouth—at today's antique auto prices.)

By putting your boat on your car top, you save the cost of a trailer plus maintenance, depreciation and yearly licensing fees for it. Tolls with a trailer are often exorbitant. (I've found ferry boat tolls the worst. Do you suppose they are jealous?) I find it more comfortable to drive long distances with the boat overhead. A trailer always nags at your worry button.

You'll find one person can lift about one hundred pounds of clumsy boat. That adds up to two hundred pounds for two. If you go beyond that, you'll need some kind of mechanical aid. The first one to try is a roll bar. On some station wagons you can mount the aft rack close enough to the back of the roof so you can hoist the front of the boat up on it. Then you go to the stern, lift it and roll the boat forward. Since you are never lifting more than one-half the boat's weight, you can handle twice as much boat. However, many wagons slope in so much or lose their rain gutters toward the back that mounting the rack far enough to the rear to do this becomes impossible. Don't give up the ship. You are still not licked. Fasten a sidebar between the two racks. Bring the boat, bow first, to the car and lift the bow up on the side bar. Then you lift the stern and push the boat over the car. When it starts to balance, slowly and carefully turn it to the usual fore and aft position. With metal bars, it isn't as difficult as it sounds as the boat turns easily on metal-to-metal contact. With wood it is harder. And I dare say from time to time you'll scratch up your car's roof. I do—ugh!

There are other mechanical aids. West coast firms sell elaborate winch rigs that lift cartoppers up on camper tops. SEARS markets a turn rod that clamps to the bumper of your car and extends higher than the roof. You lift the stern of the boat and fasten it to the top of the rod. A fitting similar to the screwdowns that hold your outboard on keeps it there. Then you lift the front end of the boat and walk it around until it slides on the front auto-top rack. It's a pretty fair rig and would be better if made out of better stuff. The price is right—about $18.50. COSOM CORP., 6030 Wayzata Boulevard, Minneapolis, Minn. 55401, sells a better-made one for $28.50. S & P ENTERPRISES, 2603 N.E. 7th Avenue, Portland, Ore. 97208, have one of the block and tackle rigs for $195 manual, $295 electric. QUIK-N-EASY, 934 West Foothill Boulevard, Monrovia, Cal. 91016, markets their version in the $135 area.

The least expensive fore and aft racks are wooden ones with rubber suction cups. They come in around $7.50. Put a length of shock cord between the gutter straps and they won't come loose when the car hits a bump. QUIK-N-EASY make iron pipe racks with a nifty sidebar. This rack clamps mechanically to the gutter and the boat in turn is bolted to the racks. Cost is about $45 and since it is the best and safest it is the rack used in our representative boat listings.

Most racks come store-bought at around 4½ feet across but you can rig extensions easily to carry two canoes. Again, their graceful shape makes lifting aloft easy. A boat adding to a car's drag, incidentally, will chop into your gas mileage a fair amount. I've never found windage a problem despite some trips through storms. The travel trailer folks tell me the streamlining effect of a boat actually helps when towing a high trailer behind. I hope you can equip yourself like the camper I saw tooling down Florida's Sunshine Highway last winter. It was a BIG camper. On the front was lashed a Honda Trailbike. Overhead was at least a fourteen-footer. A 20-h.p. CHRYSLER hung in a bracket on the back of the vehicle, and behind was a Volkswagen in tow. This guy had everything. Boat listings are on pp. 60–63.

Johnboats

Like the common man, God must have loved johnboats. He made so many of them. If there is *the* fishing boat, this slab-sided ugly duckling is most certainly elected.

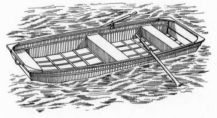

Native originally to the Mississippi, johnboats now dominate the boating scene on protected inland waters. They're just *everywhere.*

How do you decide between a cartopper or johnboat? The roughness of the water is the criterion. Pace off fourteen feet in your living room. Put a five-foot beam on it. Now, take a mid-point at one end and lead a line

Aluminum

ALUMA CRAFT BOAT DIVISION, Alpex Corp., 1515 Central A enue, N.E., Minneapolis, Minn. 55413

Model	Length	Beam	Weight	h.p.	Cost
Model EZ	12'	4'1"	110	7.5	$219
Model E	12'	4'1"	115	12	279
Model R-7	12'2"	4'7"	145	20	329
Model AZ	13'7"	4'1"	131	7.5	269
Model A	13'7"	4'1"	137	12	299
Model F 7	14'	4'7"	169	28	359
Model FD Fish	14'1"	4'7"	210	40	449

APPLEBY MFG. CO., R. R. #1, Lebanon, Mo. 65536

Model	Length	Beam	Weight	h.p.	Cost
12' V-Bot Lake Fisher	12'	4'4"	115	18	$170
12' V-Bot Lake Fisher	12'	4'4"	115	18	180
12' V-Bot Laker Deluxe	12'	4'7"	118	18	200
14' V-Bot Lake Fisher	14'	4'4"	130	18	190
14' V-Bot Lake Fisher	14'	4'4"	130	18	200
14' V-Bot Laker Deluxe	14'	4'7"	133	18	240
14' V-Bot Laker Supreme	14'	5'	200	40	235
14' Ski Fisher Runabout	14'	5'4"	250	40	495
16' V-Bot Laker Supreme	16'	5'	230	40	369

Aluminum

DURATECH MFG. CORP., Wadell Avenue, Penn Yan, N.Y. 14527

Model	Length	Beam	Weight	h.p.	Cost
Viking Fish	12'	4'8"	110	10	$241
Viking Fish	14'	4'8"	130	10	278
Fisherman Open	14'	5'5"	170	30	360
Fisherman Open	15'8"	6'	240	40	470

STARCRAFT CORP., P.O. Box 577, Goshen, Ind. 46526

Model	Length	Beam	Weight	h.p.	Cost
Cartopper	11'	4'8"	89	6	$177
Sea Scamp Fish	12'	4'4"	126	10	210
Super Star Fish	12'1"	4'9"	151	15	245
Falcon Runabout	14'	5'6"	390	40	625
Sea Scamp Fish	14'1"	4'5"	142	20	245
Super Star Fish	14'1"	4'9"	185	20	299
Seafarer Fish	14'2"	5'3"	215	25	330
Seafarer Fish	16'	5'5"	280	35	390
Star Trek-V	18'	5'10"	315	60	995

Aluminum

MONARK BOAT COMPANY, P.O. Box 210, Monticello, Ark. 71655 (MonArk)

Model	Length	Beam	Weight	h.p.	Cost
MonArk SV-12 Semi-V Util	12'	4'4"	125	10	$180
MonArk SV-14 Semi-V Util	14'	4'4"	140	18	200
MonArk UT-14S Semi-V Util	14'	4'10"	195	24	300
MonArk UT-14D Semi-V Util	14'	5'	205	35	320
MonArk Pro Rnbt	15'	5'4"	200	40	495
MonArk UT-16 Semi-V Util	16'	5'3"	225	40	365

SEARS ROEBUCK AND CO., Chicago, Ill. 60607

Semi-V 12 Cartopper	11'6"	49"	87	10	$168
Semi-V 14	13'7"	53"	111	14	225
Heavyweight 14	13'6"	63"	155	24	299
Semi-V 16	16'2"	72"	257	35	319

Fiberglass

CROSBY AEROMARINE CO., Marianna, Fla. 32446

Model	Length	Beam	Weight	h.p.	Cost
13 Crosby Sled	13'3"	5'6"	270	40	$440

Fiberlass

MFG., 55 Fourth Avenue, Union City, Pa. 16438

Car Top Fisherman	12'1"	4'4"	125	10	$232
Challenger Fisherman	14'3"	4'6"	175	20	280

HERTER'S, INC., Waseca, Minn. 56093

Model Canada	12'	50"	145	10	$194
Model Resorter	14'	55"	160	16	216
Model Alaska	14'	62"	190	30	273
Model Yukon	16'	68"	235	40	346

SEARS ROEBUCK AND CO., Chicago, Ill. 60607

Game Fisher	12'	50"	125	14	$198

four feet back on either side. Leaves a nice point, doesn't it? Also discards a good portion of the boat too. This is how you make up your mind. Are the waters where you'll use the boat rough enough so you can casually throw away one tenth of your boat? If so, choose a car-topper. If not, a johnboat is the logical purchase. You may have noticed that there is a boat getting lost here—the traditional flat-bottomed rowboat, a sharp-bowed johnboat if you want to call it that. Apparently it offers so little more seaworthiness than a regular johnboat most people aren't willing to sacrifice the boat space. In any case, it's getting harder and harder to find one.

It's true that johnboats have their limitations. Throwing water around in a chop is only one of them. Someone wrote me recently that he'd used a johnboat for years on a local river and loved the doggone thing. Then they dammed up the river to form a huge impoundment. "It was okay at first," his letter went. "The boat was fine. But now whenever it gets windy I go over one wave and under the next. How can I catch fish when I'm always bailing?"

Usually the trouble is that someone transports a boat to waters for which it is unsuited. But in this case, the character of the water changed from sheltered to open and took the poor unsuspecting johnboat by surprise.

The bluff johnboat bow gives you plenty of room, but can't cut through waves and throw the water aside, the flat bottom and square ends don't move up and down in the water easily. Don't forget, for one end of a boat to rise to a wave, the other end has to sink. Old John, he stays put, come what may. If you push his capabilities too far, you may find yourself swimming.

But it is just this stay-put ability that makes a johnboat the great fisherman it is. You can sit on the side of a johnboat and the johnboat won't care. It stays put. Two men can stand up in one and flail the water furiously with fly rods and Old John stays put. If you float a stream for ducks and a mallard with an I.Q. of 160 lets you go past before he jumps, you can swerve violently around to miss him. The johnboat will stay put.

All this stability comes from a combination of two factors: flat bottom and beam. Which brings another star attribute of johnboats into view. They can handle horsepower in quantity and go like blazes. Perhaps no other hull so efficiently uses the push of a motor.

Here are some speed tests run on MonArk aluminum johnboats at the MERCURY OUTBOARD proving grounds:

The first boat is 14 feet 1 inch long, weighs 150 pounds, is made of .064-guage aluminum and has a 52-inch beam at the gunwale and 32-inch bottom width. The boat is a relatively heavy commercial model.

Motor	Gross Weight (pounds)	Speed
3.9 h.p.	377	10.9 m.p.h.
6 h.p.	385	14 m.p.h.
9.8 h.p.	382	23.1 m.p.h.

The second boat, also a commercial fishing model, is 16 feet long with 69½-inch beam, 48-inch bottom width and a hull weight of 240 pounds. It too is heavily framed and is built of .072-gauge aluminum.

Motor	Gross Weight (pounds)	Speed
9.8 h.p.	472	20.4 m.p.h.
20 h.p.	530	29.5 m.p.h.

The really significant thing is that the first boat is rated for 18 h.p. And the second at 35 h.p. With that power both vessels would run easily at speeds above 35 m.p.h., and that gets you home in a hurry.

What plenty of people don't know is that johnboats can be long, graceful craft rivaling the canoe for ease in slipping through the water. The famous OZARK johnboats were originally thirty feet long with a scant twenty-five-inch bottom width. Newer boats built for tourist floats are twenty feet long and still only thirty-four inches wide on the bottom. These are wooden boats and are paddled by the guide aft. In fact, they won't take much more horsepower than a canoe. The drive of the motor will cause the stern to sink, there isn't enough lifting surface there to handle high power.

You can put the principles involved in the difference between the two kinds of boats. If you plan to paddle or row your boat, try to find a long slim boat. If you will use a good size motor and want speed, look for a beamy vessel. I'll admit, though, that modern production lines don't give you too much choice.

The johnboat lends itself to a type of fishing prevalent through the south. There, one man sits in the stern and sculls the boat along. One hand works a cane pole, dropping a worm in every likely stump pocket or weed tangle, the other weaves the paddle back and forth in figure-8 fashion. The paddle never leaves the water. An even better way to fish a johnboat is to mount an electric motor up on the bow. The instantaneous response of an electric motor plus its silence gives you exact control over the boat's motions. Many electric motor companies now offer remote controls you operate with your foot. Both throttle and steering can be controlled with the remote unit, yet both hands are free to fish. What won't they think of next? Johnboats to think about are listed on pp. 68–70.

Accessories and Special Gear

There are a number of special gimmicks you can put on a little aluminum boat to make it more livable. First among these, in my opinion, is an extension handle for the outboard. This is just a long handle that attaches to the outboard steering arm and gives you steering and speed control three feet or so from the motor. This allows you to get your weight up forward where the boat balances out. No doubt you've seen these boats running along with one man in the stern and the bow scraping the clouds. Keeping the "V" of the bow in the water makes for softer going in rough water, makes the boat faster and keeps it under much better control. Most extension handles are adjustable in length and they snap

APPLEBY MFG., Lebanon, Mo. 65536

Model	Length	Beam	Weight	h.p.	Cost
8' Custom Jon	8'	3'10"	65	5	$ 89
10' Thrifty Jon	10'	3'4"	62	3.5	69
10' Custom Jon	10'	3'10"	70	7.5	99
12' Thrifty Jon	12'	3'4"	68	5	89
12' Cust Jon	12'	3'10"	80	7.5	129
14' Cust Jon	14'	3'10"	90	10	149
14' Jon (extra wide)	14'	4'6"	140	18	229
14' Big Fish Jon	14'	5'10"	200	20	329
16' Jon (extra wide)	16'	4'8"	160	18	269
16' Big Fish Jon	16'	5'10"	260	30	369
18' Jon (extra wide)	18'	4'8"	180	20	299
18' Big Fish Jon	18'	5'10"	280	35	399

MONARK BOAT COMPANY, Box 210, Monticello, Ark. 71655

Model	Length	Beam	Weight	h.p.	Cost
Cajun 1030 Fish	10'	3'9"	70	4	$ 90
Cajun 1230 Fish	12'	3'9"	80	6	115
Scout 1232 Fish	12'	4'	100	6	150
MonArk 1258 Fish	12'	4'	105	10	175
Cajun 1430 Fish	14'	3'9"	95	7.5	130
Scout 1432 Fish	14'	4'	130	10	180

MONARK BOAT COMPANY, Box 210, Monticello, Ark. 71655

Model	Length	Beam	Weight	h.p.	Cost
MonArk 1458 Fish	14'	4'	140	18	203
MonArk PN-1458	14'	4'	130	18	215
MonArk 1464 Fish	14'	4'8"	165	20	240
MonArk 1448 Com Fish	14'	5'10"	240	20	335
MonArk 1452 Com Fish	14'	6'4"	285	30	410
MonArk 1664 Fish	16'	4'8"	190	25	285
MonArk 1648 Com Fish	16'	5'10"	260	35	385
MonArk 1652 Com Fish	16'	6'4"	325	35	475
MonArk 1848 Com Fish	18'	5'10"	280	35	445
MonArk 1852 Com Fish	18'	6'4"	365	40	535
MonArk 2048 Com Fish	20'	5'10"	300	40	495
MonArk 2052 Com Fish	20'	6'4"	400	50	597

OUACHITA MARINE, Box 420, Arkadelphia, Ark. 71923

Model	Length	Beam	Weight	h.p.	Cost
12EE John Boat	12'	3'4"	60	3	$104
12E John Boat	12'	3'10"	72	5	121
12S John Boat	12'	3'10"	96	10	146
12-17 John Boat	12'	4'2"	112	10	178
12DW John Boat	12'	4'6"	126	10	206
14E John Boat	14'	3'10"	93	10	140
14L John Boat	14'	3'10"	186	10	161

OUACHITA MARINE, Box 420, Arkadelphia, Ark. 71923

Model	Length	Beam	Weight	h.p.	Cost
14-17 John Boat	14'	42"	140	15	212
14-16 John Boat	14'	42"	145	15	221
14DW John Boat	14'	4'6"	156	18	240
14DW40 John Boat	14'	4'6"	160	18	240
14SDW John Boat	14'	5'10"	204	25	359
16DW John Boat	16'	4'6"	176	18	276
16SDW John Boat	16'	5'10"	224	35	391
18SDW John Boat	18'	5'10"	252	40	448
20SDW John Boat	20'	5'10"	275	40	500

SEARS ROEBUCK AND CO., Chicago, Ill. 60607

Model	Length	Beam	Weight	h.p.	Cost
Jon-10	9'9"	47"	71	5	$ 94
Jon-11	11'9"	46"	75	7.5	108
Jon-13	13'11"	48"	85	7.5	127
Jon-14	13'11"	55"	132	14	177
Jon-15	15'10"	70"	242	30	335

off in a second if two persons are aboard and the helmsman wants to assume his regular seat aft. Another use of
the extension handle is that it allows you to run the boat
standing up, important if you want to look ahead or
peer around for signs of fish. HERTER'S, INC., Waseca,
Minn. 56093, sells a handle for $6.45.

On boats fourteen feet and larger it is easy to install
remote throttle and clutch controls and a station for
wheel steering. Usually these go aft—about two thirds of
the distance between the bow and stern. A kit costs
about $25. Good canvas shelter tops that fold out of the
way can be rigged over such a control station. Also available are clear drop curtains that can be snapped in place
all around. Such small shelter cabins aren't being used
as much as they should today on little boats. The art of
the canvas maker has advanced greatly. It's no trick to
completely protect the helmsman from the elements. Yet,
a few snaps and the whole cover folds out of the way.
Cost of the fold-down top is about $85. Clear forward
and side curtains would add another $75.

Portable seats with back rests fit neatly on rear thwarts.
The old timers love them as they can sit sideways comfortably all day long and troll.

A lot of people object to the noise of aluminum boats.
This can be dampened with rubber floor mats available
at any auto supply store.

Standard equipment in any open boat is a good plastic
garbage can with screw-down lid. I take binoculars,
walkie-talkie, foul weather jacket and spare sweater,

lunch, flashlight, small tool kit and matches. In other words, everything I want to keep dry. I leave it right in the boat. Trailering, two lids blew off until I got smart and tied them on. The lids screw down well enough to be water- but not wind-proof.

If you trail all the time, permanent running lights are no problem. If you sometimes cartop, permanent lights could catch on car racks. I meet this problem with battery operated running lights and a removable white stern light. I drilled holes so I can bolt them on and take them off when need be.

Sailing
Surfboards

The man stood there shaking his head. "Used to be sailing a boat had some dignity to it." As he spoke, a tiny lateen rigged vessel sizzled down the 30 m.p.h. wind, slammed over in a jibe and promptly tipped over. "Look there," the man lamented. "Now all of them will tip over." He was correct. Boat after boat swept down on the race marker and one after the other upset. Not for long. Crews were righting them as fast as they went over and scooting on their way. "It's not a sailing race," the man moaned. "It's a righting contest." Suddenly he turned to me and his face broke in a wide grin. "You know something? It looks like a heck of a lot of fun."

This conversation or something like it (it was blowing too hard to hear well) actually happened. The man was an old friend of mine and a sailing buff from way back.

I knew a Sailfish regatta was scheduled in our area and when the day dawned with scudding grey skies and 30-knot winds I figured some excitement would be in store. I wasn't wrong.

If I erred in my prediction it was on the conservative side. Frantic was the only way to describe the response of the boards to the massive gusts of wind. The Super Sailfish has plenty of sail to make it "hot" under normal conditions. When the stiff breezes got behind them, the little boats would surf down waves as if their skippers suddenly cut in jet afterburners. Clocking 15 m.p.h. was nothing out there that day. No one could keep count of how many capsizes the fleet endured. But fun! You could see the enthusiasm on the faces of the boys and girls and men and women who were fighting it out for first place. They were wet, of course; cold, probably, and tired they had to be. But still smiles, shouts of pleasure and an air of gaity permeated the regatta. It was fun to be a part of and, if the size of the crowd watching was any indication, as entertaining as it was exciting.

While I think a canoe is the most boat for the buck, ever since the first surfboard sailed into my ken in the early 1950s, I've maintained they had to offer the most boating *fun* for the buck. It is almost designed into them. The little boards are all fun. In a canoe or even a one-design sailboat you can get into grueling situations; for example, long uphill paddles or sudden squalls. With the boards you don't set sail unless conditions are comfortable. Bathing suits are the uniform of the day for all; this limits you to warm weather boating. Since even the best of them are uncomfortable for extended sails, most of the boards get used for brief periods with rests in between.

These limitations will appear in the negative column later when we take a hard and stonyhearted look at boards in general, but they have served an important purpose. I feel the boards have made an inordinate contribution to the revival of sailing interest that swept the boating world in the 1960s for just this reason: They display and dramatize the joys of sailing.

A couple sailing past in a conventional deep-hulled one-design boat certainly look as though they are having a good time. But not quite in the same way as a board sailor. He or she is more likely to leap out of the water onto the boat and dash away. The girls are screaming, the dogs are barking and convulsions of laughter sweep the spectators when a capsize occurs. It's going too far to suggest that a sailing surfboard is only one more step down the beach ball, rubber float and plastic bathtub route. Nonetheless they have a symbiotic relationship with swimming. And people only go swimming when it's fun. It is as simple as that.

People worry about conventional sailboats with their intimidating jargon and ever-present threat of an embarrassing capsize. The boards do away with the latter and ignore the former. More than that. They capitalize on weakness and make upsets a nifty part of the game, like being sent back to GO If you don't know how to sail—so what? There is only one rope to push or pull on—whichever you do—and the stick in the back makes the front go in the desired direction more often than not. If it won't, paddle home. That's fun too.

ALCORT INC., who are still chairmen of the "boards," have earned their prime position through sound maneuvers. While a Sailfish or Sunfish looks simple, it ain't by a long shot. The hull form is an extremely complicated shape. More than anything it is responsible for the boat's amazing performance. (When it first came out the Super Sailfish was one of the fastest sailboats afloat. Even after a decade of developing super fast one-designs, they can still hold their own in fast company.)

From the very first, the boards delivered on performance. But the second shrewd thing ALCORT did was not compromise on quality. They built their boats to last and priced them accordingly. Even today they aren't cheap in relation to their size, yet the boats stand the gaff. They take the beatings that it is so much fun to give them. Better than any other boat they fill a specific niche in the boating world, and you don't need this pundit to convince you of that. Sales of some seventy thousand Sailfish and Sunfish alone are better proof.

I doubt if anyone can go far wrong buying a sailing surfboard. Resale is prompt and they hold their value like rocks. You can anticipate twenty per cent depreciation a year and this makes bearable numbers if you find the boat doesn't please you. Nevertheless, I think you should look deeper than the façade of all that fun we

were talking about before you leap. Let's take a look
at both sides.

Advantages

The little boards are all light and any of them can be
easily cartopped. Beam in the four-foot range makes
cartopping two boats difficult without special rigs. Most
people pull two boats on a small trailer rigged with an
upper and lower arrangement.

The boards can be carried around as easily as a canoe
and can be rigged (i.e., the rudder attached, the sail
hoisted) in seconds. All are super-simple to sail and because of the near impossibility of doing harm to themselves or anyone else make excellent junior sailors. The
boards are also good for rough water sailing as tipping
over is a little more than a nuisance and the boats slice
through big waves. Unswampable and unsinkable, they
are extremely safe and, as has been pointed out, the boats
can be paddled surfboard style for miles without fatigue.
Since they knock down instantly and must be transported
that way, storage presents no problem. In cellar or garage
they can stand on their side throughout the winter and
take up little space. Hanging from the rafters in a
garage is another good way to store them. Fiberglass
boats require little maintenance beyond annual waxing.
Aluminum masts and Dacron sails likewise take care of
themselves. The sail should last ten years unless you are
racing, in which case a couple of seasons will probably
be all you can expect and still stay out in front. (Win-

ning one-design sailors consider themselves lucky to get
one season out of a suit of sails.) Mahogany rudders and
centerboards will probably get scarred and will require
touch up sanding and revarnishing annually.

Disadvantages

The disadvantages of the boards are obvious. They
are bathing-suit-only boats. As such they confine themselves to warm days. Since you have to get wet to launch
one and a capsize is a certain eventuality, the water better be warm as well. Of course, you can wear a skin
diver's wet suit and sail all winter long. The kids now
surf through the winter wearing wet suits. This begins
to get somewhat heroic, however. Nevertheless, a wet
suit top might be considered to extend your season and
increase the number of sailing days. Cost of just the top
is around $35 at most sporting goods stores.

Almost all boards employ a dagger board instead of
the more usual centerboard. The difference is that when
a centerboard hits something it is merely pushed up
into the centerboard trunk. The dagger board backs
against the hull slot and the boat stops. Like RIGHT
NOW! It is also more difficult to sail the dagger board
in shallow water as it can be pulled up only so far until
it starts to become an unwieldy obstruction. In water
about two feet deep you can pull the board up enough
to still retain windward ability but not very much. I'd
guess in any wind above moderate it would be well to

figure a minimum draft of 18 inches. Most people over-look this fact, but the boards for all their small size and convenience are relatively deep-draft small boats. If you must sail in very shallow water this is a definite point to consider.

For kids, sitting guru style is no great hardship but I can assure you after a while an adult's legs and rear end begin protesting this strange style of locomotion. That there are some thirteen thousand members of the Sun-fish Association and only six thousand Super Sailfish members attests to the comfort afforded by the small but critically-positioned cockpit of the Sunfish. It allows you to sit in a more normal and hence far more comfortable position. If you tip over, hulls of cockpit boats are de-signed to float high enough out of the water so the cock-pit doesn't fill.

Racing

A great positive advantage to the sailing surfboards is that you can race them today in regattas all over this country, as well as Europe and Central and South Amer-ica. In March or April the ALCORT people mail to regis-tered owners a list of all Sailfish and Sunfish fleets operat-ing in this country and abroad. There are some two hundred four. Included is a list of all regattas scheduled by these fleets and their dates. The races start in May and end in December. International meets are reported as they become known. Members haul their boats to domestic regattas but for international races only the sails go along. Boats are provided by host clubs. And you can imagine for yourself the hospitality that would be shown to a visiting sailor under these circumstances. If a wealthy South American says, "come be my guest," he means for several months!

Racing has its drawbacks. In general the trend of one-design racing has not pleased me. It is overly scientific, overly expensive and requires an over-commitment, either you must go whole hog or not at all. I am sure that if you compete in the Sunfish Nationals you'll find winning skippers are exacting perfectionists, dedicated up to if not beyond the point of enjoyment, and advanced theorists in what makes one sailboat go faster than another. Yet insofar as board boats are concerned, the excitement of a regatta and the fun of participating more than make up for it. To me, it makes more sense to pour money into a boat costing $500 than one costing $5000. Even a small new Blue Jay or Comet will set you back $1600 and these are the *least* expensive racing machines. Your Sunfish or Super Sailfish, the only boards *widely* raced, is a fun machine that can race if you feel like it and that makes all the difference.

I'm going to give some opinions on the differences between the boards I am familiar with. Yet I'd buy a board on the basis of the race fleets available to you. In many parts of the country, local fleets of Glaston or Starcraft boats, for example, are undoubtedly racing. Armed with the proper boat you have not only a fun-in-the-sun sailor but an invitation to a new kind of party. It just isn't that difficult to join a race group, sail the marks and enjoy the company of other owners. Even if you wind up sailing your best to escape last place instead of secure first place you'll have a ball. The racing capability adds a new dimension to any sailboat's potential. Even if you personally never plan to utilize it, the potential will be reflected in the boat's resale value. Where racing is concerned the rule is the more the merrier. If your sailing surfboard becomes an entree to new friends and new fun, my allegation that the boards return the most fun for the boating buck will be engagingly true.

A few notes about the following listings are in order. No one will ever list all sailboats in any publication that has a time lapse of more than several hours. The life span of many boating companies duplicates that of the May Fly, which lives and dies in a single day. New hopes surge models forth, old and unfavorable profit and loss statements cause others to silently fade away.

Prices are manufacturer's published prices and tend to enlarge as the proximity of a dealer's showroom increases.

I have some opinions about which sailing surfboard to buy. If you are cautious about it (or broke) get a Sea Snark and try it. The guy who sells it to you will be glad to take it in trade if you want to trade up next season. If you want more class than the Snark affords, or more performance, look at the boats racing near you. If fleets of other boards are in action, buy one of those. If there are none, I'd recommend going with the originators and going for the Super Sailfish or Sunfish.

SAILING SURFBOARDS AT A GLANCE

ALCORT INC., Box 1345, Waterbury, Conn. 06720, is the manufacturer.

The Sailfish came first. In 1948, as a matter of fact. It is still offered in kit form only.

Marine Plywood Kit

Boat	Length	Beam	Sail Area	Hull Wgt.	Crew Capacity	Cost
Sailfish	11'7½"	31½"	65 sq. ft.	82	200 lbs.	$224 *

The Super Sailfish with slightly more length and beam but a much greater sail area in relation to the hull is thus a "hotter" boat and is offered in two forms:

Factory Finished Fiberglass

Super Sailfish	13'7"	35½"	75 sq. ft.	98	400 lbs.	417 *

Marine Plywood Kit

Super Sailfish	13'7"	35½"	75 sq. ft.	102	400 lbs.	254 *

* All prices include Dacron sail and aluminum spars, rudder and centerboard. Fiberglass boats have white hull, choice of deck colors.

Adding a cockpit increases beam, weight and comfort. The beam becomes important because it enables the boat to carry more sail and be slightly less tippy. Called the Sunfish, it comes in two versions:

Sunfish	13'10"	48½"	75 sq. ft.	139	500 lbs.	537 *

Factory Finished Fiberglass

Boat	Length	Beam	Sail Area	Hull Wgt.	Crew Capacity	Cost
Marine Plywood Kit						
Sunfish	13'7½"	47½"	75 sq. ft.	142	500 lbs.	$328 *

Scorpions manufactured by FIBERGLASS DIVISION, Columbia Car Corp., 220 Dalton Avenue, Charlotte, N.C. 28202, have almost identical specifications with Sunfish and in some areas are allowed to race with Sunfish.

Boat	Length	Beam	Sail Area	Hull Wgt.	Crew Capacity	Cost
Scorpion	13'9"	47½"	75 sq. ft.	140	500 lbs.	525 *

* All prices include Dacron sail and aluminum spars, rudder and centerboard. Fiberglass boats have white hull, choice of deck colors.

CHRYSLER BOATS, Box 2641, Detroit, Mich. 48231, has two sailing boards. Both fiberglass with cockpit.

Boat	Length	Beam	Sail Area	Hull Wgt.	Crew Capacity	Cost
Cat Rig						
Barracuda	13'3"	54"	95 sq. ft.	180	600 lbs.	700 *
Lateen Rig (like Sunfish)						
Barracuda	13'3"	54"	88 sq. ft.	180	600 lbs.	665
Man 'O War	15'	54"	—	—	—	799

GLASTRON BOAT, Box 9447, Austin, Tex. 78756, has a cockpit version.

Boat	Length	Beam	Sail Area	Hull Wgt.	Crew Capacity	Cost
Fiberglass						
Alpha	15'	49½"	98 sq. ft.	170	500 lbs.	$625

SNARK PRODUCTS, 1580 Lemoine Avenue, Ft. Lee, N.J. 07024, offers a bathing suit boat (it isn't quite a board) made out of a polystyrene foam-like substance that is more rugged than you might suspect. Although somewhat crude, the amazing price includes a Dacron sail. I suspect several seasons of normal wear and tear would probably leave the boat battered beyond recognition. It, nonetheless, is a real sailing hull, no bathtub toy, a truly remarkable boat for the money.

Boat	Length	Beam	Sail Area	Hull Wgt.	Crew Capacity	Cost
Sea Snark	11'	38"	45 sq. ft.	62	500 lbs.	115

THE O'DAY CO., 168 Stevens Street, Fall River, Mass. 02722, makes a full line of fiberglass sailing boats and was one of the first in the fiberglass day sailor business. They offer two sailing boards, both fiberglass.

Boat	Length	Beam	Sail Area	Hull Wgt.	Crew Capacity	Cost
Swift	10'4"	38"	44 sq. ft.	80	400 lbs.	335
Super Swift	12'8"	3'8"	80 sq. ft.	120	500 lbs.	495

ALUMA CRAFT, 1515 Central Avenue, N.E. Minneapolis, Minn. 55413, has a fiberglass board with aluminum dagger board and rudder.

Boat	Length	Beam	Sail Area	Hull Wgt.	Crew Capacity	Cost
S-12	12'	48"	75 sq. ft.*	178	500 lbs.	505

* 20 sq. ft. jib optional, $50.

▶IV

Vest-Pocket Sailors

It was my last cruise and it meant a lot to me. As a matter of fact, it still does. Time has not dimmed the adventure.

I was heading for the army. It's a worrisome time for any youth. You know different and dangerous experiences lie ahead. The uncertainty of it all leaves you uneasy and there's only one thing you can be sure of. A boy leaves and a man returns. As the boy is left behind, so are the special pleasures of youthful days. I wanted to take the very best with me. I wanted a last fling.

My boat was a fourteen-foot Penn Yan sailing dinghy, a lovely thing, handsomely shaped, light yet strong, stout in a sea and lightheaded and responsive on all points of sail. Her age and mine, eighteen, about meshed. We were close friends, that little vessel and I. Our friendship was born of much cussing, hard work and exhilarating joy. The best kind.

I loaded the dinghy with pup tent, assorted camp and forage gear and headed down the bay. I knew a place. There was a grove of pines that stuck out into the bay. I knew the pines would shelter my tent, yet the daily southerly winds would sweep the point clear of bugs. They'd keep me cool. It was a perfect place to make my camp.

When the first light broke I'd rout soft-shelled crabs out of the thick eel grass. Crabs not quite ready to shed went in the live box. As the afternoon shadows lengthened, they were bait for my hook and, as a result, fat weakfish and succulent flounders sizzled over my camp-fire. Days were reserved for exploring. My little dinghy, with its tip-up rudder and champagne-glass hull lines that required but a suggestion of centerboard to keep on course, opened each cove and natural harbor to me. When grub ran low, I'd tack up a long meandering river that held a state marina and grocery store at its head. As I threaded among the yachts, tourists would gape in wonder that a boat could sail like that. The old timers knew days when the only horsepower was sail power and sailboats went everywhere. They smiled and waved.

When the time ran out there was a fair wind. As I sailed away from the past, it freshened as if to carry me on my way. I sped the length of the bay and tied my dinghy to a boat broker's dock. A check for $150 was all I ever saw of it again.

Twenty years have passed since then. There have been a succession of bigger boats, but none better. Pollution has ravaged the bay I cruised on, but there are many more bays, unspoiled and alluring, that you can speed to with your boat on a trailer or car racks or maybe just slipped in your station wagon. The chapter on "Boat Camping" will go into detail on what you need to do to equip your boat for this kind of zestful combination of boating and camping.

But you don't have to camp to make your boat spin out the stuff dreams are made of. A memorable story in *Yachting* magazine some years ago told of a young couple who headquartered in a motel in South Carolina and explored the intriguing out-islands there in a Penguin, no less. Their experience was matchless; so cheap and so rewarding, with real stick-to-the-ribs memories. Here's what the author said at the end of his trek.

"What I love about boats is the look of them slicing through a head sea or running like great birds. And the places they take you and the thoughts they make you think. And letting yourself be cradled in the wind's arms. And the strength and danger and eternal verities they allow you to share. If ever my boat seems unduly small, it cheers me to remember that I've experienced more joy in one afternoon aboard a Penguin at Hilton Head than ever I knew on a voyage across the Atlantic and back in a vessel 600 feet long."

Isn't that charming? And I can assure you it is true. This sailor braved high winds and bad weather. He even had a storm sail for the Penguin. His daily voyages required skill and the lonely area added danger to the equation. But I must add that his boat, much as he loved it, was poor for this work. You'll find a dozen listed that are ten times better and can take you where he went in much greater comfort and safety.

And, let me ask you this: How many places within a day's drive would you like to explore just like this couple did? Well, what's stopping you? If you camp it will probably cost less than staying home, because you supplement the budget with wild foods. If you stay at friends or in your camper-trailer or in a motel or tourist house what could a week cost you? Maybe $10 a night for two if you splurged. Just as with the sailing boards, you should test your sailing ability against others in regatta races because racing is convivial and exciting. But unlike the sailing boards, with your sailboat you aren't a slave to warm weather. Your boat will keep you dry. It will carry extra loads from lunch and a thermos of coffee on up. And since most of the boats we'll list draw less than 8 inches of water with rudder kicked up and the board drawn, the doggone thing will take you almost anywhere it is wet.

Perfect small sailboat country is a sheltered bay about a day's sail long (twenty-five miles), an hour's sail wide (three miles) and dotted with coves, islands, hidden harbors, picturesque villages, marinas and anchorages full of other boats to study. Among sailors Boat Watching is taken as seriously as Girl Watching. The sport reaches its obvious zenith in Girl Watching Aboard Other Boats, especially so since the combination of sun and privacy seem to encourage the scantiest of bikinis.

I can guarantee if you stayed in a motel in Oxford, Md , you could sail every day and never see the same sight twice. Also on the Potomac and among the islands of Newport Bay on the St. Lawrence or the San Francisco Delta. Camp in the Land Between the Lakes and two huge impoundments are your oyster. It would be easy to go on forever. Across our land dozens and dozens of suitable sailing areas await penetration by intrepid and fearless explorers, like you.

"But what if we tipped over?" This is the first question that comes up when you start talking about sailboats. Sailboats do tip over. Just like cars smash into things.

If the fatal moment comes and over she goes, you find out why every sailboat is made to float. You climb up the high side of the hull and await rescue. In crowded waters, an overturned sailboat draws help like a magnet. People worry about getting caught trapped under the sail. This would be extremely hard to manage even if you worked at it. As the boat capsizes, passengers tend to be thrown on top of the sail, not under. If you did get under the mainsail, you'd just push it aside in the small boats we are talking about.

But even if you tipped over and help is nowhere, you can right the boat and bail it. Any book on basic sailing describes the several techniques.

The main answer to the question is that you really don't have to tip over. I'm no better a sailor than thousands of others. Here's my record by boats:

Boat	Years Owned	Capsize
Gunning Box	4	No
15-foot Racing Sneakbox	4	Once (100 feet from the dock)
14-foot Sailing Dinghy	3	No
16-foot Comet	4	Twice (racing in violent conditions)
11-foot Penguin	3	No (despite an extremely nasty dismasting in high winds)
12-foot Sneakbox	4	No
30-foot Bugeye	4	No (thank God)
14-foot Blue Jay	2	No
18-foot Marshall Catboat	½	Not yet

With the exception of the Penguin, which is a hot little boat, all those craft were normal, fairly stable vessels. Yet all were fast and responsive except the gunning box which wasn't meant to be. Most dinghies today are designed with kids in mind. All have generous beams. What this does is increase the stiffening effect as the boats tip. If you never, (did you get that NEVER) let me repeat myself one time for emphasis, NEVER, NOT ONCE, EVEN FOR A SECOND! let the sheet out of your hand so you can let it fly just by relaxing your grip, you won't tip over. Hopefully. Probably.

I'm reminded of my instructor in basic artillery training, who said, "This 105 howitzer shell is what they call bore safe. It cannot go off, until it has been projected from the mouth of the cannon. An amazingly effective safety device renders it absolutely harmless in the condition in which you now see it." He paused ominously. "Don't drop one anywhere near me, though."

There are any number of good basic sailing books that you should read if you are just starting. *Learning to Sail* by the grand boating writer H. A. Calahan is a great classic, although showing its age in the modern materials sections. A brand new book by my friend Monk Farnham, *Sailing for Beginners,* rectifies that and Monk writes as entertainingly as he "racontoots" (isn't that what a raconteur does?) Both are widely available. Another classic available in paperback is Bill Wallace's *Sailing.* I might interject that sailing is like riding a bicycle. Once you get the hang of it, you're home free on the whole bloody lot of them. In fact little boats are harder to sail than big boats. Big boats are more forgiving. If you make a mistake, they have enough mass and inherent stability to keep on an even keel. The little fellows demand attention RIGHT NOW! Even then it may be too late. The foregoing need not apply where docking is concerned. You decide which boat you'd rather have smash into your dock—the one hundred-foot schooner America or an eight-foot dinghy.

"But aren't these sailboats you talk about awfully small?"

Answer: Frankly, yes. This will be the only area where I succumb to temptation. Yet you can load about four hundred fifty pounds of weight—human or otherwise—

in about twelve feet of boat. I am 6'3" and I've curled all that body in many a dinghy and you can too. I will readily admit being physically small is a great asset around boats. Midgets have it the best of all. Since we aren't bound to the $1000 maximum by federal law, I'm going to include in the specifications section some really nifty little day sailors that exceed that figure by a reasonable amount. You can save the difference by reading this book in a library, for example. Of course, you very well might save the whole amount by not reading it at all. But what a dull clod you'd be.

"What's the difference between the sailing dinghies and board boats? After all, the board boats *can* be righted easily if you tip over. Isn't that an advantage?"

Answer: Yes, but for this you trade off some other advantages. The most obvious is that by staying dry you greatly extend the use of the boat. Several of the boats we'll look at are what they call "Frostbiters." They are raced all winter long whenever waters are free of ice. Not only do the dinghies and day sailors carry you in comfort, they can lug along ice boxes, water jugs, picnic lunches, extra clothes and so forth. Another plus is the fact that they can be equipped with the smallest type outboard and made into a small auxiliary.

"If we wanted one of these sailboats, what is the minimum size we'd need? We are a family of four."

Answer: Boats get bigger by the cube of their size. As they get longer, they are also becoming deeper and broader. To help get some understanding of capacities let's separate the small sailors into three categories.

Tenders

These will range from seven to nine feet. There are plenty of styles since most owners of larger sailboats tow a tender, or take it on deck if the big boat can handle it. All the tenders are fiberglass and amazingly enough some of them sail moderately well. Some, it must be added, are poor performers. At best they must be considered one-adult boats under sail. Even an eight footer will float three adults and can be rowed in calm water with this load. Yet to ask the boat to move so much weight gracefully is too much. Even with two adults (three hundred pounds) the average sailing tender is overburdened under sail. Since we are talking about taking at least two adults and some equipment on our cruises, we'll consider only the next three categories.

Small Day Sailors

The term day sailors is one of the few boating expressions that make sense. It describes a boat aimed at taking several people out comfortably for a day's sail. Many day sailors are lovely little things and as tough and able as they are pretty. Lengths will be from about ten to perhaps thirteen feet. In this size we'll come in around our magic dollar figure, often including a modest outboard as well, and the boats will be dandy for two people. Because families are involved and there are so many excellent choices in the family-sized fifteen and sixteen-footers, we'll extend the budget upward to include a couple of these.

One-Designs

This classification includes all boats built in a given class that must conform to fairly rigid specifications. The intent is to make all boats the same. Only very slight differences from boat to boat are permitted and always a minimum weight is specified. Before you can race in any big-time competition you must locate an official class measurer and he will measure and weigh your boat and certify that the class standards have been met.

Today with so many fiberglass boats coming out of the same mold, many sailing dinghies and even tenders are being raced as one-designs, just as board sailors are. The term has come to describe mostly racing machines because this is the direction one-design racing has taken. Almost every item on these boats is adjustable. Mast rake and position, sheet location, traveler pull and so forth are adjusted constantly for maximum efficiency in different winds and points of sail. Exotic gear bristles from them.

Because weight, or the lack of it, is so important to a racing boat, most one-designs today are what they call "dry sailed." They go in the water prior to a race and come out after it. Their captains don't permit them to soak up moisture and add weight. Even a fiberglass boat will absorb some moisture in the flotation.

Oddly enough there seems to be somewhat of a trend toward small one-designs of very advanced design. Most racing machines are so gussied up with special gear that they exceed our $1000 mark by a wide margin. But the little fellows come in well under the mark and we have included them in the "Sailboats That Sizzle" section.

Large Day Sailors

There are beauties aplenty in this classification. I'd love to talk about some seventeen and eighteen-footers that actually offer real sleeping accommodations and sea-going ability. Alas. We are way over the budget (times two or three) with these so we will try to blot the whole idea out of our minds. Remember, though, you can't be jailed for what you're dreaming about.

If it was apparent that the hard-working, beleaguered writer of this book had problems trying to catalogue dozens of local canoe builders, you should know something about the sailboat biz. A man could spend his life stalking new classes of sailboats, and at the end he'd be no better off than when he started since dozens would have sprung up in his footsteps. Almost every body of water big enough to qualify for the title has spawned its own breed of racing sailboats. For a time it appeared that the character of boatbuilding was changing. Only larger manufacturers, it was thought, could afford fiber-glass molds. Now it doesn't seem so well pronounced. Local builders have turned more and more to fiberglass and one thing about boatbuilders you can depend on is they will be independent of thought, word and deed, and totally convinced they are right and that their boat excells all others by an unreasonable amount.

Often they are right, God bless 'em. You will find hundreds of small sailboats all over the country that this pundit never heard of. As in the case of the sailing boards, I strongly suggest following local custom. If a type of boat is popular in your area and fits your purpose and price, buy that kind even though another boat may seem more attractive. The blessings of this action are multiple. First, if fleets are racing you can join them, or your kids can if you don't want to. Nothing is quite so forlorn as a one-design far from home. You may know it for a great boat on certain waters, but in strange territory it is out of place and may well be too deep or too tender for winds and water for which it was not in-tended. The boat will not sell as promptly when the time comes. Nor will it retain its value as well. Deprecia-tion will be higher.

The boats listed in most cases represent designs that are aimed at national markets. They are generally able to handle whatever conditions they may find. However, if active fleets of any are operating near you, urge your-self in that direction. You won't regret it.

As sailboats get larger and more sail plan options are

available (i.e. genoa jibs, spinnakers, etc.), prices are usually quoted less sails. Our boats are mostly small enough so a main and jib are standard. Prices quoted include those. Light sails like the above would be extra. Much equipment is extra—anchors, seat cushions, special jam cleats or winches—but the price should include all running rigging, sheets, halyards and stainless standing rigging and the rudder and centerboard. Prices do not include a trailer, which would run in the $150 range for these boats, or an auxiliary outboard, which would add another $100—$150.

Many small boats offer what is termed roller reefing. This is a positive advantage and every small boat should have it, especially those that plan to join our employ. What this does is roll the sail up on the boom like a window shade. The less sail, the less the boat tips. When it is calm you use all the sail; if the wind picks up to where the boat is continually overpowered (i.e., trying to tip over all the time) roll up some of the sail.

The differences in rig enter this picture too. A cat rig has one sail, so does the lateen rig favored by the boards. But the sloop rig flies a main and jib. By thus dividing the sail into roughly one third and two thirds it enables you to reduce sail in a jiffy merely by lowering the jib, or if it's *really* blowing, the main. For potting around the cat rig is okay but if you are serious about small sailor cruising I'd favor a sloop and I'd want roller reefing too. If you love the cat, have reef points sewed into an old sail you don't use for racing.

The O'DAY CO., 168 Stevens Street, Fall River, Mass. 02722, holds a commanding position among sailboat manufacturers. The company was one of the first all-fiberglass builders. Additions to their fleet have been sane, well-built, encouraging boats. The company's determined promotion during the dark days before sailing surged helped keep the spark alive in the minds of many. During these times I helped organize a firm devoted solely to selling small sailboats. A man bought a Rhodes 19 built by O'DAY and we said we'd deliver it by water about ten miles away on the next weekend. "But maybe the weather will be too bad," the chap said. My partner and I looked questioningly at one another, for neither of us knew of any hurricane in the offing. It is a real tribute to that boat that literally only a hurricane could have kept us from sailing his boat down the bay. If a regular old garden-variety gale had blown in, we'd have donned foul weather gear, reefed her down and had a magnificent sail. So can you.

The O'DAY CO. has an excellent catalogue worth perusal. Prices not included. (They are afraid we can't take it, I guess.) They do offer free propaganda-type sailing literature. Ask for it. Here are three of their boats I like. All three are raced as one-designs in many areas.

Sprite: Length, 10'2"; Beam, 4'9"; Hull weight, 150; Draft, board up, 3", board down, 3'5"; Sail area, 63 sq. ft.; Price, $695 to $795. The Sprite has a convertible feature in that it can be sailed as a catboat for simplicity's sake when used as a trainer. The mast can be moved aft to change the rig to sloop rig with the addition of a jib. The Sprite will handle two adults with some crowding. Kick up rudder, spinnaker available. Light enough to cartop.

Widgeon: Length, 12'4"; Beam, 5'; Hull weight, 250; Draft, board up, 5", board down, 3'6"; Sail area, 90 sq. ft.; Price, $1040 with sails. The Widgeon is a handsome little sailor, small enough for kids, but able to handle two adults with some comfort. Has kick up rudder for beaching. Can fly spinnaker. Still cartopable with two men.

Javelin: Length, 14'; Beam 5'8"; Hull weight, 495; Draft, board up, 6", board down, 3'10" (a keel version with a draft of 24" is offered); Sail area 125 sq. ft.; Price, $1595. This boat extends beyond the reasonable weight limits for cartopping so the cost of a trailer must be added to our price extension. The keel version would be difficult to trail. The boat will handle an outboard up to 7 h.p. and motors in this range sell for $300. Nevertheless this boat with its small shelter cabin so perfectly fits our measure of a small cruising ship that the author, a notoriously weak man where little boats are concerned, has included it. The keel version would be almost impossible to tip over. Roller reefing is standard. Cockpit space is almost ten feet and the Javelin will gobble up a family of four and still not be affected by the weight.

Kick up rudder and centerboard retain full shallow water capability. Spinnaker. Good storage. A peach of a little cruiser.

The MFG CO., Union City, Penna. 16438, is a large boat manufacturer holding a commanding position in the small outboard market. Their sailboat division has a fine boat.

Pintail: Length, 14'; Beam, 6'; Hull weight, 350; Draft, board up, 6", board down, 4'; Sail area, 122 sq. ft.; Price, $1445. They call this boat a fine family sailing craft and it will handle two adults and a couple of kids with some crowding. Yet the hull has handsome lines and ample sail area to make her fast and responsive. An able little cruiser. Kick up rudder. Spinnaker. Storage area.

CHRYSLER MARINE PRODUCTS, Box 2641, Detroit, Mich. 48231, offers a nice small sailor.

LS-13:   Length, 13'1"; Beam, 61"; Hull weight 350; Draft, boards up, 7", boards down, 3'; Sail area, 93 sq. ft.; Price, $1170. Two special features to LS-13. First is twin centerboards, which are slightly more efficient if you use them correctly, but in the opinion of many, including this Boats Editor, more trouble than they are worth. A better feature is an enclosed storage area under the bow, which can be locked, with a removable panel and good storage areas under seats.

STARCRAFT BOATS CORP., Goshen, Ind. 46526, is the largest small boat builder with extensive national distribution. They have a design that deserves mention.

Seaflite 12: Length, 12'6"; Beam, 58"; Hull weight, 310; Draft, board up, 5", down, 38"; Sail area, 78 sq. ft.; Price $650. The Seaflite is little more than a junior trainer although it allegedly will carry 450 pounds. Twin hull configuration.

CAPE DORY CO., 373 Crescent Street, W. Bridgewater, Mass. 02379, offers two hulls with traditional lines. Both resemble my sailing dinghy mentioned at the beginning of this chapter and the fact that they are fiberglass instead of cedar and canvas is something we can all be thankful for. These boats are truly delightful little vessels and smart sailors. I'd welcome either in my stocking Christmas morning.

Cape Dory 10: Length, 10'6"; Beam, 49"; Hull weight, 150; Draft, board up, 5", board down, 24"; Sail area, 68 sq. ft.; Price, $575. A sweetheart but on the small side.

Cape Dory 14: Length, 14'6"; Beam, 51"; Hull weight, 200; Draft, board up, 6", board down, 36"; Sail area, 85 sq. ft.; Price, $775. Prices are with nylon sail. Dacron sails add $20 but are well worth it. Both boats employ a sliding gunter rig (one sail) which keeps the heavy part of the mast low and a lighter sprit mast high. This makes the boat slightly stiffer. The lateen rig of the sailing boards accomplishes the same thing except the gunter rig is not penalized on one tack by the sail flattening against the mast. It is a good rig for a small boat and can be reefed like a cat if reef points are included. Both these boats, or any small sailboat for that matter, can be rowed easily for hours because the hull must be able to slip through the water with little effort. However, few manufacturers equip their boats with oarlocks, perhaps because they feel it breaks the spell. Since these dories come up through a tradition which saw rowing vessels first to which an auxiliary sail was added, they have rowlocks in two positions. If you think two good men on two pairs of oars can't cover five miles in a half hour in the fourteen-footer, don't place any substantial sums behind your opinion. The boats also handle a small outboard as auxiliary power.

There are a number of popular one-design sailors that can be raced, cruised and enjoyed for our price if you stretch it hardly enough to notice at a fast glance. May I digress amidst all this technical information to talk about money and boats. Little boats don't cost a great deal after the initial purchase because you do most of your own work, store the boat in the backyard, and so forth. Big boats cost plenty, and continue to cost. Boat yards are uniformly poor. It is very difficult to find a place where satisfactory work can be done at a given time at any price, much less a reasonable price. This has given rise to the old saying that a boat is a hole in the water lined with wood into which you throw money. I always felt my big boats were like avenging gods of old. They need frequent monetary sacrifice to keep them appeased. Without it they grow restive and belch fire. The late Al Loomis, dean of the delightful boating writers, used to say he'd open the yard bills on Hotspur, his beloved cutter, look at them with his eyes closed and hand them to his wife to pay. She had instructions never to mention the matter after that. All wives are not so accommodating, however.

Here are some popular one-designs that meet our specifications and are in wide use in various areas of the country and the world, for that matter. A word of explanation is in order. The designs previously described were boats developed, built and promoted by individual manufacturers. These one-designs that follow mostly evolved as a class and various builders have come to specialize in making them. With the previous group of vessels, the best way to learn more about them is to send for literature from the builder. But in the case of a few of those on the next pages, few of the builders are large enough and maybe it is fair to say smart enough to bother with such trivia as descriptive folders. The best way to investigate the subject further is through the class secretaries who may or may not be steadfast at their posts but will usually offer some advice on which builders are active in that class at that particular time.

Cape Cod Mercury: Length, 15'; Beam, 5'5"; Draft, board up, 8", board down, 39"; Sail area, 144 sq. ft.; Price, about $1600. The most expensive boat in our fleet, nevertheless they are so perfect for family cruising in addition to being fast and able racing boats, they earn a place. CAPE COD SHIPBUILDING CO., Wareham, Mass. 02571, makes them. Literature available.

Dyer Dhow 12½: Length, 12'6"; Beam, 5'; Draft, board up, 6", board down, 28"; Sail area, 72 sq. ft.; Price, $1150. This is a famous boat from a famous firm and in wide use along Long Island Sound. A nine-foot version is priced at $605 and has high acceptance among ocean-racing and cruising circles where it is used as a tender to the big boat. Another version comes in at ten feet and $799. All three are popular Frostbiters around the Sound. Plenty of good literature available free from THE ANCHORAGE, 57 Miller Street, Warren, R.I. 02885.

El Toro: Length, 8'; Beam, 3'10"; Draft, board up, 3", board down, 1'9"; Sail area, 38½ sq. ft.; Price, about $500. These ugly little rascals have over 5000 registered hulls and are extremely popular on the west coast. For kids mostly, though. A number of builders; address the class secretary, Mr. Kenneth Bradley, 2820 Telegraph Avenue, Berkley, Cal. 94705, for a list. In fiberglass or plywood. Kits available.

OK Dinghy: Length, 18'1½"; Beam, 4'8"; Draft, board up, 7", board down, 36"; Sail area, 90 sq. ft.; Price, about $1000. A popular west coast boat. Address class secretary,

Mrs. Judith Herrigel, 1420 39th Avenue, E. Seattle, Wash. 98102, for list of builders.

Penguin: Length, 11'5"; Beam, 4'8"; Draft, board up, 4", board down, 48"; Sail area, 72 sq. ft.; Price, about $800. Cat-rigged and originally made for easy building out of plywood; fiberglass construction is now allowed and is far superior. These are hot little buckets, and really get fine-honed in competition. They will carry two adults in some degree of comfort. Most commonly cartopped and the transom would handle a minimum outboard. Address class secretary, Mrs. Ella Leighton-Herrmann, 1217 Fourth Road, Baltimore, Md. 21220, for list of builders.

Turnabout: Length, 9'8"; Beam, 5'3"; Draft, board up, 2", board down, 24"; Sail area, 60 sq. ft.; Price, about $750 fiberglass, $525 plywood. This is one of many boats described as the minimum boat that still sails reasonably well. Excellent as a kid's trainer with simple cat rig. Too small for adults, but thousands prove me wrong daily. PARKER RIVER MARINE, Route 1 at Parker River, Newbury, Mass. 01950, has literature.

▶ V

Sailboats That Sizzle

WARNING: A CATAMARAN ACCELERATES VERY RAPIDLY AND CAN SAIL OUT FROM UNDER YOU—IF YOU ARE NOT CAREFUL OR READY. SO HANG ON!

Those ominous or exhilarating words, depending on your point of view, are included in an instruction booklet offered by a leading catamaran manufacturer. Do you believe that an unaware person can be sitting in a sailboat and a puff of wind can shoot the boat right out from under him or her? Read the warning. Does it give you pause that sailboats are surfing down giant waves in Hawaii and southern California? (It should. Those surfers gotta be crazy!) Do you yearn for a sailboat in which you can sally forth on a brisk, breezy day looking

106

for high-powered outboard boats that you can race against AND BEAT! Step right up friends, you're at the right counter.

You will remember how we said it was high performance that "made" the first sailing surfboards. They really went. And still do. My sailing dinghy wasn't slow. It would clock seven knots on a beam reach and smoke would rise from her wake. Any of the day sailors and one-designs we mentioned are what you must term "high performance" sailboats. They are very fast, extremely close winded, exceptionally responsive.

Then you know what kind of boats we are talking about when we say the sizzlers make them all look like antiques. In winds of any velocity the sizzlers would sail right past the conventional boats as if they were anchored. Literally! In a 20-m.p.h. wind, they can clock 20 m.p.h. or close to it. Writers especially prone to sailboat joys are fond of pointing out that going 6 m.p.h. in a sailboat seems as thrilling as going at five or six times that speed in a powerboat. And it is true. A sailing vessel near hull speed strains to leap ahead. Spars groan, sheets are hard, the rudder is alive in your hands.

What is it like when a sailboat goes three times that 6 m.p.h. maximum? You can imagine. It is a sensation unlike any other. The waves fly by, the sound of the hull knifing through the water is a high-pitched hiss. When puffs of added wind velocity strike, the boat does not first heel, then speed up. It leaps ahead like someone jabbed it in the rear, and keeps going. If you want to get technical, the reason regular sailboats have a maximum speed is they push water aside. The faster they go the more energy is absorbed making waves. This is why at slow speeds so little effort makes them go. No energy is spent making waves. It all contributes to speed. The new boats are radical departures from this age-old law. They make a bow wave . . . then climb up on top of it and stay there! They plane on top of the water just like an outboard. Many one-designs will do this. So will the sailing boards if conditions are right. Conditions don't have to be right for the sizzlers. That's the name of the game for them.

Coupled with radical hull designs—either multi-hulls (catamaran or trimaran) or mono-hulled versions—comes a Pandora's box full of speed gimmicks. Full length battens that hold the shape in the sail whether there is wind or not: dynamic hull configuration, vangs, adjustable stays and mast positions, bendy masts often unstayed, and many, many more. Some are obvious, many not so apparent. Each subtle maneuver adds its fractional amount of extra power until the whole thing is a great big sizzling bomb.

The disadvantages of the boats are apparent. They are frantic to sail, demanding, and hard work. Sailing one taxes both alertness and muscles since you are always hanging out over the side trying to keep the boat sailing flat. Even in the smaller sizes where expense does not exceed our maximum, an advanced theoretical knowledge of the dynamics of sailing vessels is necessary to extract anywhere near the best the boat is capable of. The boats could not be classified as strictly bathing suit sailors. It *might* be possible to stay dry if you pick a calm day. However, it doesn't make much difference. Skippers and crews are prone to wear heavy sweaters which they soak. With the upper parts of their bodies water-laden they keep the boat flatter when they hike out. One west coast crew member was drowned when he fell overboard. It was found he had *lead* in his shirt. See what I mean about one-design mania?

Yet with all of it, there is undeniable glory here. Part of it is being best, the fastest, first. Another important element is the thrill of soaring over the water with such intensity. It is the ultimate under sail, the greatest challenge to skipper and boat. Brain and brawn are tuned to the peak.

A word of explanation on hull configuration is in order. When the multi-hulls came into public view, they captured everyone's imagination. Since the three hull configuration of a trimaran doesn't lend itself to the smaller sizes our budget restricts us to, we can set them aside. The catamarans were—and are—fast, but not simply by virtue of hull shape. Off the wind, the twin hulls may be slightly faster than a mono-hull. Climbing up the wind, I daresay a mono-hull has the edge. The important thing is the efficiency of the whole boat. The whole bag of tricks. A really tuned mono-hull will wipe a slow cat's nose. And vice versa. You'll find the catamarans harder to capsize than a mono but they offer their own nasty little idiosyncrasies. Samples: They dig in the leeward hull and submarine. They are slow, even laborious, to bring about. Straight before the wind (running) they are snails. Skippers tack downwind to keep the wind abeam and keep, or try to keep, the whiz-bang speed. When and if a catamaran capsizes, it is slightly more troublesome to right. A nauseating affliction is to tip all the way over with the mast hanging straight down, or more likely stuck in the mud. A catamaran is not necessarily faster or less prone to capsize than an equally efficient mono-hulled vessel.

Another point to consider about the sizzlers is that unlike the sailing boards most have a conventional centerboard which, with tip-up rudder, makes them able to sail in more shallow water.

These boats are too new and too hot to have many racing fleets in action as yet. However, if there is racing in your area the buy-to-race principal applies. I would also view used boats in this category with great suspicion. Strain on gear and hull are obvious and considerable.

Sidewinder: Mono-hull. Length, 15′3″; Beam, 4′6″; Hull weight, under 200; Sail area, 108 sq. ft.; Price, $1120. British design. Loose-footed main which may be rigged as cat or sloop. Two position centerboard. This boat is brand new. A long, narrow bomb. Distributed by and information from MFG CO., 55 Fourth Avenue, Union City, Pa. 16438.

Catfish: Catamaran. Length, 13'2"; Beam, 72"; Hull
weight, 190; Sail area, 105 sq. ft.; Price, $1100. This is
an ALCORT INC.'s bid for franticism. They claim (and I
don't doubt that they've clocked it) 18 knots! The
Catfish is all rigid fiberglass, well-constructed. Not quite
as souped up as some sizzlers, emphasis is on the family
fun side. ALCORT offers an excellent book describing the
characteristics of catamarans in general and the Catfish
in particular. If you disguise yourself as a prospect I'm
sure you can corral one free. Address ALCORT INC., Box
1345, Waterbury, Conn. 06701.

Flying Fish: ALCORT also fields a mono-hulled sizzler.
Length, 14'; Beam, 5'8"; Sail area, 120 sq. ft.; Draft,
board up, 4"; board down, 2'10"; Hull weight, 190
pounds; Fullbatten Dacron sail and bendy mast. Price,
$1100.

Aqua Cat: Catamaran. Length, 12'2"; Beam, 6½'; Hull
weight, 160; Draft, board up, 5", board down, 24"; Sail
area, 78 or 90 sq. ft.; Price, $850. This boat too is ad-
vertised as being clocked at 18 knots. Can be cartopped
on VW's. Nylon sail. A pipe frame connects the two
hulls in this boat, canvas stretched between makes the
cockpit. This is an odd-sounding arrangement but more
comfortable than you'd suspect. AMERICAN FIBERGLASS
CORP., Box 2466, Norwalk, Conn. 06856, is responsible.

Flying Saucer: Mono-hull. Length, 15'; Beam, 5'2";
Hull weight 195; Draft, board up, 6", board down, 3'3";

Sail area, 115 sq. ft.; Price, $1045. Expect O'DAY not to let the grass grow under his boats. Self-tending jib on his sizzler (so hands are free for important work . . . like hanging on). Bendy rig that automatically adjusts sail shape. Fiberglass gull-wing hull that planes in 12 knot winds. Exceptional performance in light winds with two people. (There are those midgets again.) Address O'DAY CORP., 168 Stevens Street, Fall River, Mass. 02722, for further details.

Bonito: Mono-hull. Length, 14'6"; Beam, 4'; Hull weight, 100; Draft, board up, 6", board down, 2'5"; Sail area, 88 sq. ft.; Price, $645. Dagger board on this one, Bendy mast, unstayed cat rig. Designed by designer of one-man Olympic racer, the Flying Finn. Looks like a smaller version of this bombshell. LINCOLN FIBERGLASS, Gleasondale Industrial Park, Route 62, Stow, Mass. 01775, is an American distributor for this British built boat.

Cheshire Cat: Catamaran. Length, 13'6"; Beam, 6'6"; Hull weight, 198; Draft, board up, 5", board down, 25"; Sail area, 135 sq. ft. (Wow!); Price, $1150 including sails and trailer. This is a racy-looking cat with full batten main and jib of Dacron. Roller reefing. Rotating mast. CATAMARAN SAILBOATS, Route 4, Box 248, Old Raleigh Road, Durham, N.C. 27703, has the full frenzied story.

For some reason people who admire catamarans and

trimarans seem to like to build their own. GLEN L. MA-
RINE DESIGNS, 9152 E. Rosecrans, Bellflower, Cal. 90707,
has two sailing cat kits at twelve and fifteen and a half
feet.

Inflatables

Few people today know that the story of inflatable boats starts with lives being saved in the North Sea more than twenty years ago. For years fishermen aboard English, French and German trawlers depended on conventional small boats as lifeboats in the event of floundering in the wild storms of the area. Too often the small boats quickly swamped. Even if they remained afloat loss of life from exposure was severe.

It was found that rubber life rafts similar to those developed for flyers in World War II were far superior to the boats as life saving vessels. They took up less room on the trawler, remained afloat even though swamped and could easily be provided with a full tent-like canopy to shield crews from the cruel winter elements.

It took much demonstration and convincing to get the fishermen to give up their traditional craft. As I recall, the Royal Navy got into the act. But gradual acceptance came about and put a number of firms in business making the new craft.

Since then I have watched the transformation of clumsy life rafts into high-speed motorboats with great admiration. In the better inflatables, rubber has long been discarded in favor of harder-wearing synthetics, a proliferation of designs to meet all kinds of needs has taken place and public acceptance has been satisfactory. Indeed, it has actually lagged behind the opinion of the professionals. Most of the long-range expeditions today are employing inflatables instead of canoe-like craft. One twenty-four-year-old English secretary actually took a nine footer across the English Channel and cruised it one thousand miles through the canals of France.

We are getting all this history and flavor of foreign lands not merely to permit the Boats Editor to reveal his dazzling knowledge (although it's about time) but to point up the two most salient characteristics about most inflatables you can buy. Basic to the breed are:

Foreign Manufacturers

With a couple of exceptions almost all of the manu-facturers of inflatables are European—French, English or German. The boats are in much wider use through-out Europe than in this country. Americans tend to view

with some suspicions products from abroad but I can
assure you that is not justified in the case of these little
vessels. Some are better than others, of course, but all
I have examined, and I think I've examined most of
those distributed in the United States, seem built to high
standards with much thought and care.

Rough-water Ability

Any inflatable is a dozen times safer in raging rough
water than the best small boat. The reason can be
summed up in one word—buoyancy. Extreme lightness
combines with great lift. Even swamped inflatables remain upright, ride high out of the water, can be controlled and readily bailed out. This factor has made
them favorites with the river shooters. On many of the
western rivers in national parks, float trips are permitted
only in inflatables. Not only does the inflatable's super
buoyancy keep it always afloat, the cushioning rubbery
sides slide harmlessly away from rocks that would oblit-
erate a conventional craft. Anyone who has shot rapids
in a canoe knows how important it is to steer clear of
the rocks. In an inflatable it doesn't make any difference.
The boat will bounce away from any within reasonable
limits.

There are several obvious advantages to inflatables.
The ability to store a relatively big boat in a relatively
small space is first among them. The little Avon is a
favorite with the city-bound cliff dwellers. Anytime you

can moor a boat in your closet or haul an eighteen-footer totally within the confines of a Volkswagen bug you've got a good thing going.

Backpackers love boats that blow up. They hike into hidden, remote and secret fishing places with the boat deflated. At the bank they install the air and create havoc with the fish population. Since they weigh little more inflated than empty, the boats can be carried easily even full of air.

Lots of skippers of big boats prefer the inflatables for tenders, not just for the safety factor. They are far safer than the usual pram in the event of a floundering. The same buoyancy that keeps them afloat in river rapids serves equally in the open ocean. Another not so obvious benefit is that the inflatables don't scar up a boat hull when they nudge against it. It is hard handling even a light fifty- to seventy-pound tender back and forth over a big boat's side without busting or scratching something. Not so with the balloon boats. Here is some quick inflatable information:

What Are They Made Of?

The better boats use nylon cloth covered by a synthetic rubber like neoprene. They are impervious to gasoline, sunlight, heat. Life of the good ones should be five to ten years. Punctures are fixed like a flat tire with a cold patch. Abrasion can be a problem. Stop it by glueing a canvas (or neoprene) section over the vul-

nerable area with a flexible waterproof glue like Good
Year pliabond.

Rubber Boats

SEARS, MONTGOMERY WARD and mail order houses carry
rubber boats for $40 or less in two-man versions. These
are rubber on cotton cloth, probably made in Japan and
are okay for the price. But water quickly rots the cotton
cloth and heat, sun and gasoline quickly deteriorate the
rubber. They are especially susceptible to ozone in the
air. More than a four-year life is improbable IF you
don't get a boat that has been overly long on someone's
shelf where it will deteriorate without any help from
anybody. Once deterioration starts I know of no way to
halt its steady advance. To prolong life, keep them cool
(cold is better), out of sun, sprinkle with talc, fold as
little or as loosely as possible. Scrub off any gas spill with
detergent. Waxing them with a hard non-petroleum base
wax helps.

Performance

All inflatables handle poorly under oars or paddles.
Winds blow them around something fierce. You can't
tow them over about 8 m.p.h. behind a bigger boat or
the wind will flip them. Any is much improved with a
plywood floor that can be made removable.

Safety

All the good boats are made in at least three different and separate air chambers. Usually storage can be neatly accomplished by deflating only one section and folding this section into the other.

Blow Up

Air pressure carried in the boats is low—about two pounds per square inch. Lungs can make this and work okay for the smaller size boats. Most boats issue a hand or foot pump to help make it easier on you. It takes around ten minutes pumping to get most boats hard. Also like any air filled object the doggone critters can get perverse. You blow them up in the hot sun then launch them in cold water and they deflate slightly when the air contracts. Most manufacturers offer a CO_2 bottle attachment that will do the blowing for you. These are relatively expensive and mostly designed for emergency use. There are various devices that hook to a car motor to blow them up and save your lungs.

Assembly

Like most things, assembling the inflatables I've had some experience with isn't all wine and roses. You have to lay the boat out on its lines, free everything and see that the right things are started in correct positions.

Times given for this by the manufacturers in the specifications are certainly minimums. Also the little balloons
don't deflate readily. Forcing and squeezing the air out
is like getting into a necking contest with the circus fat
lady. If you start to enjoy it, see your doctor.

Speed

Most of the boats beyond the backpacking class can
handle a motor to 3 h.p. and go pretty well—6 to 7 m.p.h.
In a wind they can be true-blue dogs to steer. I once
put on an exhilarating performance back of Barnegat
inlet trying to put an eight-footer alongside my cruiser.
I'd turn the motor but the boat would skate merrily on.

A removable plywood floor enables any inflatable to
use the power much better. Also makes the boat much
more comfortable. You can step into it, for example.
Only the fabric floor supported by water makes walking
precarious.

High speed inflatables are somewhat new. What manufacturers have done is mount a full wooden floor and
tie the transom into this so the thrust of the motor is
contained. This makes the boat much more complicated.
Also, if you are calculating closely don't forget the
knock-down size which I have listed is for just the boat.
Floorboards and transom in the high speed boats make
another bundle as big or bigger than the fabric. Remember too that hitting a sharp rock at 5 m.p.h. is probably okay but at 20 m.p.h. you'll rip the fabric.

Maintenance

Hose with fresh water before folding. Occasionally sprinkle with talcum powder. Fold only in very loose folds and watch that sand or small stones have not gotten between the side compartment and floor. Best long range storage method is to partially inflate and keep in cool, dark place. Especially guard against rodent predation. Rats and mice will chew heck out of them.

Disadvantages

These are manifest. The boats look and somewhat act like an overgrown hot dog. They are bulky, cumbersome, clumsy and ugly. They are cranky to paddle or row, lacking all semblance of underwater lines. Even the best cannot be considered long-lived compared to fiberglass or aluminum boats. While by no means as vulnerable to tears and punctures as they used to be, both these hazards remain and are certain to insure your local service station of getting some patching business from time to time.

Nonetheless, for all their faults think how foolish you'd feel trying to fit a canoe into your apartment elevator, or a Sailfish, or a fourteen-foot outboard. Or any boat but an inflatable.

Here is who makes what:

AVON: Probably the leader in the field with excellent distribution. Boats are British made and sold through a number of importers in this country. The main ones are INLAND MARINE CO., 76 East Jackson Street, Wilkes-Barre, Pa. 18701; IMTRA CORP., 11 University Road, Cambridge, Mass. 02138; SEAGULL MARINE SALES, 672 South Lafayette Park Place, Los Angeles, Cal. 90057. AVON offers a good booklet called *Inflatable Dinghies— Your Questions Answered,* which is worth extra study as is their catalogue. All free from any of the above. Models are listed on pages 123–125.

A great many of the extremely large rafts you see in television movies of shooting the Colorado, etc., can be obtained only through surplus government equipment. The operators glue heavy canvas over the bottom. I have had some experience with surplus material and it is a dangerous world. Decidedly you want to thoroughly examine anything you purchase. One of the oldest and most reliable firms is SURPLUS TRADER CORP., Box 8, Thomasville, Pa. 17364. Their catalogue lists 12-man rubberized nylon, CO_2-inflated-only rafts $15' \times 6'$ with canopies and assorted gear at $179. They also list a limited quantity of twenty-man rafts. This is the only place I know where these huge rafts can be obtained. Prices are quoted on demand and (I assume) according to condition.

Another French firm, ZODIAC, puts out a line of extremely rugged inflatables and the biggest commercial model that I can find. This is a giant nineteen-footer capable of taking 80 h.p. A new United States distributor should make it easier to find out more about these boats.

Name	Inflat. Size	Stow Size	Weight (lbs.)	Capacity	Motor	Assembly Time	Spd.	Appr. Price
Red Start 8 ft.	8' × 4'	33" × 18"	33	2-3	3 h.p.	4-6 min.	5-6	$280
Red Crest 9 ft.	9' × 44"	40" × 18"	40	4-5	3 h.p.	4-6 min.	5-6	320
Red Seal 10 ft.	10' × 48"	43" × 20"	45	5-6	4 h.p.	6-8 min.	5-6	375
Red Shark 12 ft.	12' × 4'10"	43" × 20"	52	6-7	5.5 h.p.	6-8 min.	7-8	425
Sportboat S-60	9' × 50"	43" × 20" × 11½"	66	2	6 h.p.	8 min.	10	400
Sportboat S-100	10½' × 58"	51" × 20" × 12"	97	3	10 h.p.	10 min.	17	460
Sportboat S-250	10½' × 58"	51" × 20" × 12"	97	3	25 h.p.	10 min.	22	595
Sportboat S-400	12½' × 66"	57" × 24" × 13"	137	4	40 h.p.	15 min.	31	695
Sportboat S-550	14½' × 74"	63" × 26" × 14"	194	6	55 h.p.	20 min.	28	830
Sportboat S-650	16½' × 82"	68" × 28" × 14"	247	10	65 h.p.	30 min.	30	995

A French firm, LIDAIR, also offers an intriguing line with emphasis on different models, including some cute beach toys that will keep the small fry working while you play. Their catalogue is well worth study and is obtainable from Mr. Guy Rabion, 1128 North Water Street, Milwaukee, Wis. 53202. First boat is a perfect backpacker, the Samoa, a double-ended kayak, 10'8" × 37", folds into 13" × 20" package weighing 20 pounds. Takes no motor but can carry a crude sail. $159.

There are three more conventional inflatables.

Name	Inflat. Size	Stow Size	Weight (lbs.)	Capacity	Motor	Assembly Time	Spd.	Appr. Price
Flores	10'4" × 4'2"	40" × 18"	52	2-3	5 h.p.	10 min.	5-6	$295
Tania	9'2" × 4'	40" × 17"	60	2	5 h.p.	10 min.	5-6	235
Viti	9'8" × 4'11"	48" × 26"	75	3-4	10 h.p.	15 min.	12	450

SEARS lists three inflatables in their catalogue. They are rubber on cotton canvas and made in Japan. They are illustrative of what this kind of boat should cost, weigh and so forth.

Name	Inflat. Size	Weight	Motor	Speed	Price
2-Man	6'10" × 4'	28	No	—	$41.88
4-Man	10½' × 5½'	42	3 h.p.	5-6	56.88
6-Man	11½' × 5'	50	3 h.p.	5-6	69.88
8-Man	13½' × 6½'	65	3.5 h.p.	5-6	99.50

A Florida-based firm specializes in life rafts. They inform me they do not intend their rubber-coated nylon rafts for anything but emergency use but they have a variety of sizes in light weights that earn them a place here. The company is the WINSLOW CO., Box 1507, Venice, Fla. 33595. Models are:

Size	Weight	Deflated	Inflated	Buoyancy	Price
2-Man	14½	6″ × 9″ × 17½″	3′ × 5′ × 4″	500 lbs.	$137.50
4-Man	23	8″ × 10″ × 23″	3½′ × 7′	1000 lbs.	255.20
6-Man	25	7½″ × 11½″ × 25″	5′ × 8½′	1500 lbs.	363.00
8-Man	32	7½″ × 13″ × 29″	5′ × 10½′	2000 lbs.	423.50
10-Man	45	8″ × 14″ × 30″	5′2″ × 12′	2500 lbs.	489.50
12-Man	52	8″ × 14″ × 30″	5′4″ × 14′2″	3000 lbs.	599.50

RUBBER FABRICATORS of Grantsville, West Va. 26147, is a stateside company offering two models of neoprene-coated nylon. Both are fine backpackers.

Boat	Size	Weight	H.P.	Price
Wildlifer sportboat	10′ × 3′8″	—	5	$239
Outdoorsman sportboat	7′11″ × 4′3″	42	3	175

KAYAK CORP. OF AMERICA, INC., 133 West 45th Street, New York, N.Y. 10036, also imports a line of neoprene on nylon inflatables for large and small horsepower. Here's how their line shapes up:

Boat	Size	Weight	H.P.	Price
Speedyak Jr.	8′3″ × 3′	33	3.5	$150
Speedyak 300	9′2″ × 4′	50	7.5	250
Speedyak 330	10′ × 4′2″	78	15	350
Speedyak 340	11′2″ × 4′10″	106	25	500
Speedyak 350	13½′ × 5′8″	200	50	825

Address ZODIAC, 1215 33rd Street, N.W., Washington, D.C. 20013. Their line ranges from a seven-footer at $200 to the fifteen-and-a-half-foot Mark III that will take loads to 2200 lbs., handle to 60 h.p. and sells for $868. The Mark V is 19′ × 8′, weighs some 385 pounds between boat and floorboards and motor mounts. This gigantic sausage takes up to an 80 h.p. motor with corresponding high speeds and sells for $1611. These Zodiacs are exceptionally rugged construction, I believe, the toughest there is. A catalogue decribes them.

This is by no means the end of the inflatable manufacturers. The boat show issue of a prominent British yachting magazine lists some twenty-three in all. You can send for one abroad if you want to go through the difficulties of currency and customs. The companies I have mentioned offer distribution in the United States.

Boat Camping

There aren't enough boat campers. That's the truth of the matter. Billions of dollars worth of recreation go down the drain annually. Campsites of awesome beauty lie unvaunted and forlorn. Beckoning waters are being ignored. Boats gather moss at their docks because local waters are too well-known, no longer new. The thrill is gone.

I know camping in general has been the hottest thing to hit the outdoor recreation field in recent years. Look at the number of travel trailers and campers that pass you on the highways. Yet I sail past a thousand water-front sites where there should be a gay little tent pitched, kids swimming, people waving . . . and there are only the trees and the wind and the loveliness. Somehow using a boat to haul family and camp gear back in to a campsite hasn't caught on.

Casting about for a culprit, I come up with the canoe. Everyone is familiar with wilderness canoeing where you camp for the night and push on the next day. They tend to think if you have a canoe and a place to cruise with it, you can go boat camping. They don't think of using a johnboat or the family runabout as a vehicle that will carry them into an impoundment, up a river, or out to an island in a large lake or sound.

You can approach the whole subject from two directions. We'll call them tent cruising and boat camping. The first implies that you are cruising. In this category would fall the wilderness canoe trip where you are following a pre-planned schedule and make camp at night in a different place. You can do the same with a cartopper in the islands of Georgian Bay, for example, and the boat is better for the job. Boat camping suggests using your boat to get to a remote waterfront spot where you make a permanent camp. The camp becomes your headquarters for swimming, hiking, fishing, boat exploring and sundry pursuits.

Either way it's hard to generalize because so much depends on the specific situation and your boat. If you have a small boat and a lot of gear, you might have to spend a whole day ferrying people and gear to your camp. In a modest-sized utility or day sailor, you can probably carry everything in one trip. Camp gear doesn't weigh much, although sleeping bags and such are bulky.

It's quite possible you might drive to a campsite, then use your boat to increase the fun inherent in camping out. There is an undeniable charm to life under the stars. I know a houseboat family that cruises in a thirty-footer with scrumptious stove, ice box, hot shower and all the comforts of home. They still put the boat's nose against the beach and build a fire in the evening. They like it.

Even if tent living isn't your dose of salts, you can take boat camping so much on very personal terms, I am continually amazed more people don't get more fun out of their boats by doing it. You can make a hotel, guest house or motel your permanent camp. Then each morning you set sail. Correction: Each *fine* morning you set sail. If the weather isn't right, you do something else. Maybe the extent of your camping is to land at lunch and cook. Or maybe the end of the lake or reservoir is a long day's run away. You sail up there, pitch a tent for the night, next day return.

Another novel approach owners of little boats are taking advantage of is to cruise from motel to motel. In many areas the proliferation of waterfront lodging makes this possible. Planning and reservations are in order. Or you might headquarter out of one motel for several days, then sail on to another. The variations are bound only by your enterprise and imagination.

If you are gregarious, you can pitch into national or state parks and join the crowd. Boating is a major visitor activity in more than forty National Parks today. Private campsites are a likely target. You make friends fast there and find it hard not to go back year after year.

No matter how you adjust to your preferences, the costs are refreshingly low and the rewards unusually high. There is an immense satisfaction to being on your own, carrying your own supplies, being independent. If you don't like it where you are—pack up and go somewhere else. Who knows? Maybe the grass really *is* greener on the other side of the fence.

Basic Equipment

You'll need an astonishing amount of equipment. Astonishing in that there is so little of it and the prices are so reasonable. The clothes you've got will do. Cotton pants and shirt, swimsuit, towels, sneakers, good heavy sweater, sturdy shorts, heavier in Maine or Canada. It would be wise to have a full rainsuit—coat and pants. But a poncho will do and even a raincoat IF it is really rain proof, few are.

Then you need these:

Tent

There are today dozens of tents, light, airy, bug proof, so waterproof not a drop gets through (especially when it doesn't rain) and all with self contained aluminum poles. Some are simpler than others to erect, but none is too complicated. One of the most famous mail order

camp outfitters is L. L. BEAN CO., Freeport, Maine 04032.
Here are some of the tents they offer. Prices are postpaid.
I might add these are first quality. Plenty of cheaper
tents can be had.

Draw-Tite Alpine Tents

These are a popular shell-shaped tent of patented
design, "compact, lightweight, insect and snake proof,
ventilated by wide 3-way zippered nylon netting door
and window."

Two-man Alpine: erect 5′ × 7′9″ × 48″ front height;
   folds 24″ × 7″; weight 12½ lbs; price $69.00.
Four-man Alpine: erect 8′ × 10′ × 6¼′ front height;
   folds 34″ × 9″; weight 30 lbs; price $139.00.
Six-man Alpine: erect 9′ × 12¼′ × 6½′; folds 39″ × 13″;
   weight 33½ lbs; price $159.50.

Bean's Wall Tent

These are the traditional high-sided, peaked-ridge
tents. Aluminum frame is self-supporting and guy lines
are needed only for heavy weather. Windows are nylon-
netted, floors vinyl-coated nylon. Net entrance and storm
door. There are two models.

Wall Tent No. 10: 10′ wide × 8′ deep × 7½′ ridge; 4′
   walls; weight 31 lbs; price $80.00.

Wall Tent No. 12: 12' wide × 9' deep × 7½' ridge; 4' walls; weight 37 lbs; price $95.00.

Draw-Tite Umbrella Tent

This is a totally self-contained tent. You can actually pick the whole tent up after it is erect. It can't blow down. There windows; water, bug, snake proof, vinyl floor, etc. Along with the wall tent, the umbrella is most popular with families.

No. 10 Umbrella: 9½' × 9½' × 7½' center height; folds 10" × 48"; weight 29 lbs; price $100.00

No. 12 Umbrella: 11½' × 11½' × 7½' center height; folds 11" × 54"; weight 35 lbs; price $128.00.

In addition to your tent you'll probably want a "fly." This is a light tarpaulin that creates a roof over the front of the tent, or wherever else you want it. Poles hold the four corners erect and guy lines keep it taut. It adds another area protected from sun or rain. They cost about $25. Tent life is hard to predict. MORSAN, 810 Route 17, Paramus, N. J. 07652, another excellent camp outfitter and mail order house, probably has more camping supplies than anybody, certainly more tents and sleeping bags, and good specifications on them. Their helpful, informative and free catalogue says this: "The average camper uses his tent 21 days a year. At this rate most tents last 20 years. However, if you were to purchase the same tent and put it up two or three months each season, the same tent would probably last anywhere from one to four seasons."

In addition to the tent you'll need:

Sleeping bags

Everybody is familiar with the advantage of these. Good ones cost $75, and you can lay down in the snow and sleep comfortably in them. Since you are in a tent which can be heated and are probably not camping in severe weather (who wants to?), look for bags in the $15—$35 area. A lot of times good sleeping bags can be too hot. You are sweltering in the bag, but the temperature may be too low to throw it completely off. You can forestall this situation with flannel liners. Gals like these anyway as they can take them out and wash them between jaunts. The liners add warmth and versatility. Another such item is a nylon fleece liner that adds ten per cent to the bag's warmth. A sleeping bag that is taken care of will last indefinitely like a blanket or quilt.

Mattresses

You can throw your bag on terra firma and climb aboard for the night if you're young and rugged. You'll sleep better—much better—cushioned by some kind of underpinning. Trail mattresses are polyether foam, very light, yet surprisingly comfortable. Cost is about $14. Air mattresses blow up and deflate for storage. They run in the $8–$12 range. Neat light aluminum cots lift you off the deck and can be used for outside sunning. Double-decker and even triple-decker versions are good in a tent as they stack small fry and keep most of the floor open. Costs are about $10 for the single, $30 for the double, $40 for the triple.

Stove and Lantern

You can cook over a campfire but there are so many really good stoves now, almost no one does it unless they have to. You'll cook on the two-burner stove, use the fire for companionship, warmth, gay music, smell, water-heating ability, grilling steaks or fish, baking biscuits and to keep bears away. (It won't, but that's what you tell the kids.) There are two kinds of camp stoves, those that burn white gasoline—for about $15—and those that use cylinders of LP gas (slightly simpler) for about $30. Either will last long into the future, a decade at least. You'll need a good lantern that floods the camp at night with light and here the ubiquitous Coleman lantern at about $25 is hard to beat. It too will camp with your grandchildren.

That's about it. You'll need sundry small items like flashlights for getting up at night, but most of these items are pretty much what you have around the house anyway.

Do you see why boat camping is included in this book

dedicated to sneaking the most fun out of the fewest
bucks?

Tent	$100.00
4 sleeping bags	100.00
4 trail mattresses	50.00
Stove & lantern	50.00
	$300.00

You can buy that gear, throw it into a fourteen-foot
cartopper ($350), attach thereon a 6 h.p. motor ($325),
all of it the very best there is bought at list prices, and
still escape with your fortune in excess of $1,000 intact.
And, friends, if you do, if you really put this stuff to
work, you'll be among the most fortunate people on
this earth. Let me illustrate with this true story.

I met this woman on Cape Cod where she lived in a
house that looked down Vineyard Sound. Outside the
window the enchanting Elizabeth Islands marched to the
horizon. She lived alone. Her husband was dead. She
was a stern and forbidding old woman, not giving to
wearing her emotions on her sleeve. One evening the
setting sun had turned the islands into burnished purple
dots in a inky-blue sea. She stood watching, then turned
to me.

"We camped in those islands, my husband and I. He
had a twenty-foot sailing dory. It was *all* he had. But
he loved his boat and I, too, grew to admire its virtues.
We sailed from island to island, going ashore where the
fancy struck us. We slept in a tent and cooked over an

open fire. At night we'd roll the boat up the beach."
Night had fallen, but I could see her eyes were glisten-
ing. "When we saw anyone we'd quickly get in the boat
and sail away. We spent the whole summer doing that.
I was eighteen and Fred was twenty. We'd just been
married."

I knew then that the house with a view down the
Elizabeth Islands did not happen there by chance. The
experience of long ago had never lost its savor.

Personal Gear

In addition to the basic living equipment you'll need
this personal gear. This list, incidentally, has been
checked and rechecked as a wilderness tent cruise list.
You can use it as a checklist if you are headed back in.
Obviously some items can be omitted if they are to be
had five minutes away at a general store.

Waterproof gadget bag to keep loose items from kicking
around.

Sheath knife and pocket Army knife.

Dark glasses with cord to prevent loss.

Matches in waterpoof case and/or lighter with fluid &
flints.

Maps of area in plastic carrying case.

Camera and film.

Log book and pencil.

Headnet, if sensitive to bugs. (Canada in June requires
one.)

Sun hat (reflected sun is always a problem).

2 pairs pants, one short if warm enough.

2 wool shirts or sweaters.

50 feet light braided nylon cord.

2 heavy-duty waterproof duffle bags, different colors if possible.

Flashlight, spare battery and bulb.

Sunburn cream in plastic container.

Compass.

Fishing tackle.

Knee pads (if you're canoeing).

Bug dope.

Lightweight rainsuit and hat.

Parka (new "space" parkas give warmth without bulk and weight).

2 shirts, one long-sleeve.

Leather belt (so you can eat it if starving or maybe just to be dramatic).

2 sets underwear (one long if cold weather anticipated).

3 bandanna-style handkerchiefs.

4 pairs wool socks in assorted weights.

Small Turkish towel.

Soap and soap dish.

Comb and steel mirror, scissors if haircuts will be needed.

Sewing kit, safety pins, buttons, heavy needles.

Pajamas, flannel if cold.

Bathing suit.

2 pairs shoes (camping is hard on shoes).

Washcloth.

Razor and blades (a battery electric shaver is good).

Toothbrush and toothpaste.

Toilet paper and personal items.

Aspirin, lip cream, pet medications.

Hunting or fishing license, fire or camp permits.

Tobacco and booze.

For the Boat and Motor

Oars, if possible, paddle if not, spare paddle for canoe trips.

Cushion life preserver for each person.

Bow & Stern line 50 feet, ⅜th's-inch nylon.

Bailing device.

Danforth anchor and 100 foot ⅜th's-inch nylon rode.

Spare spark plug, plug wrench, shear pins, spare propeller, extra outboard oil.

Repair Kit

If you are heading off into the wilderness, you should take materials with which to repair the boat. This depends on what your boat is made out of.

Wood-canvas boats: 2 × 3-ft. piece heavy canvas, copper tacks, canvas glue.

Fiberglass boats: 2 × 3-ft. piece glass cloth, can epoxy resin with catalyst, small rasp.

Aluminum boats: 3-ft. square sheets of aluminum,

box aluminum rivets, hand drill, countersink punch. The items listed for fiberglass boats will also make an effective temporary patch on aluminum.

When you have this package assembled, be wise and add some tools to fix other things. Experience, some of it dismal, has taught me that even new things, made of the very best material, break ALL THE DAMN TIME! This is what I throw into a separate bag.

25-ft. light seizing wire.
Roll plastic electrician's tape and "tire" tape.
Tubes epoxy glue.
Canvas glue and/or heavy needles and thread.
Screw, nail, bolt assortment.
Adjustable wrench.
Set open-end wrenches.
Pliers with wire cutters.
Piece emery cloth.
Large screw driver.

I add to the above a Swiss Army knife. These are widely popularized. Mine is somewhat bulky, but on a trip to Cape Breton I once used every blade. I find the gadget is always coming to the rescue.

For the Camp

Food.
Cups and plates.
Scouring pads and soaps.

Shovel (get the light trenching pick-shovel).

Folding saw, with hacksaw blade if possible.

.22 revolver and ammunition (if permitted).

Portable ice chest.

Cooking pots, griddle, reflector oven.

Fire grill (rocks support it).

Forks and spoons.

Can opener.

Axe and sharpening file or hatchet.

First Aid supplies (the Johnson & Johnson plastic kit is good).

Red Cross *First Aid* book.

Food Supplies and Menu

What you eat depends on what you like. Anyway you slice it, however, someone is going to have to plan out a menu in advance. Even if a general store is only a short snort away, you don't want to hang out there. You'll buy for several days at a time. Obviously, if you are headed for wilderness, what you eat is what you take. What you leave behind, leaves you hungry.

For years campers have relied on certain staples. These are relatively inexpensive, widely available and generally tolerated if not beloved by all. They also incorporate the vital multi-foods in one dish, principal of camp and boat cooks who are generally limited to two burners. Stews, things over rice, chilies, spaghetti, and, of course, if you have an open fire, nothing cooks steak or chops so well.

This is a good place to introduce so-called freeze-dried foods, as much a recent breakthrough in food processing as the tin can was in its day. They utilize water's ability to transform from a solid to a vapor without melting. Almost any food you can name, both in pre-cooked or natural form, can be processed. First the food is frozen then ninety-eight per cent of its moisture is vaporized away. The remainder is sealed against air contamination and may be kept for months without refrigeration. Soaked in water for fifteen minutes, the food regains its natural look and may be cooked and served. One brand, Wilson's Campsite, is pre-cooked. You heat water, open can, pour boiling water in, let sit for sixty seconds, pour out excess water and eat. How simple can you get? Expense is the only drawback. The most popular Campsite dishes are meat balls, pork and beef patties, $1.15 for two-person serving. Chuck Wagon brands are not pre-cooked, and their most popular beef stew, beef and rice and beef and vegetable sell for $1.50 for two-person serving. Weights are minimal; 3 ounces a serving for meats, an ounce a serving for vegetables. This, along with the fact that refrigeration is not needed, makes them first choice among those to whom weight is a problem—mountain climbers, wilderness canoeists and such. It should also be noted that the dishes that serve up whole meals with no more work than heating water keep kitchen morale at a peak. Trouble is, you won't see the new dishes and foods in older books on camping. They are too new. Here is traditional camp fare:

Dinners

Canned beef and lamb stew, canned corned beef or roast beef hash, pressed meats (Spam), canned corn, carrots, peas, canned soup, especially mushroom, which is used with meat, shrimp, chicken, fish, etc., to pour over rice, canned baked beans, dried beans (ugh!), canned chili con carne, canned spaghetti. Add to these such freeze-drieds as Wilson's beefsteak dinners (steak, mashed potatoes, gravy, whole corn), Wilson's pork chop dinner (pork chops, hashed brown potatoes, applesauce, garden beans); Wilson's hamburgers. Formerly potatoes were seldom camp fare. Now dried potatoes are available in supermarkets. Chuck Wagon offers now home fries, hash-browned and mashed potatoes in freeze dry. Rice along with "beans and bannock" is a traditional camp food.

Lunches

Any of the above. Plus canned hot dogs (add to beans), cheeses, many of which keep without refrigeration until opened and several days thereafter, peanut butter, canned ham and chicken spreads, which go well with bread if you've got it. Spaghetti and meat balls is probably the most popular quick hot lunch. If you are boondocking it, bread or crackers will be hard to keep beyond a day or two. In this case, make up sour dough bread or bannock. They aren't hard—flour, yeast, salt, sugar, water and heat.

Breakfast

Chuck Wagon oatmeal and freeze-dried milk, canned juices, V-8 and tomato juice (V-8 especially makes a great hot drink); Freeze-dried eggs (scrambled, western-style) with potatoes mentioned, coffee (powdered or new freeze-dried). Freeze-dried bacon is delicious, french toast is good if you have bread. Biscuits with good jams and jellies hit the spot.

Supplies

Dish washing detergent in plastic bottle, Mr. Clean or equivalent, powdered cleanser, Brillo pads, sunburn lotion, toilet paper, heavy-duty paper towels, napkins, cups, plates that burn up neatly after use.

For Kids

Large cans Hi-C or equivalent, Pop-tarts (starving adults have been known to eat these too), cereal in plastic, jelly—jams, Beef-a-Ronies and spaghetti, Fizzies. Don't forget toys, games, etc., for rainy days and drive to and from.

To Drink

Tomato juice and V-8, soft drinks, beer, ice tea (powdered), powdered orange, pineapple, lime juices, alcoholic beverage to suit (rum is a great outdoor drink for some reason).

Breads

Regular bread lasts only several days without going stale, the hard Italian loaves last longer. Try, too, Chuck Wagon biscuit or cornbread mix, canned brown bread (great with baked beans), the flour-water breads.

Utensils

You can use those nested pots camp suppliers sell, but your own kitchen will probably produce all you need. These are small, medium, and large saucepan with tops.

Teflon-lined skillet (get a deep one so you can make one-dish meals in it). Tea kettle. It's a good idea to add a galvanized bucket to the list. It can sit by the fire as a ready source of hot water in case someone wants to do something foolish like wash or shave. With paper plates and Teflon-lined pots the formerly very disagreeable camp chore of washing dishes and pots is considerably eased.

Where to Buy and More Information

Any item that your local supermarket can furnish, buy there. You'll never find it at a better price. There are excellent houses specializing in the mail order business of camp foods, freeze-dried foods of all kinds and canned gourmet stuff. STOW-A-WAY PRODUCTS, Cohasset, Mass. 02025, is one. Bill White has but recently brought real camp food thinking in depth to this business, and it stands as one of the most outstanding. A new wrinkle of his is to furnish a "package" week-long menu. You add certain items, mostly fresh meats, locally; his non-refrigerated ingredients fill out the rest of the meals.

Another superb mail order firm is the venerable S. S. PIERCE CO., P. O. Box 57, Boston, Mass. 02117. Their free catalogue lists ten pages of every food you can think of—and plenty you couldn't think of in ten years (fourteen different kinds of tea, papaya nectar, canned shad roe, plus all manner of succulent-sounding stews, hashes, stroganoffs, noodly-dishes and sea foods all in cans). Both can supply menus.

Previously mentioned MORSAN carries the full Chuck Wagon and Wilson's line and have a fine catalogue, full of campy things (nice Teflon-lined cook set, for example —$9.95) and much useful information including camping tips.

There are a number of books to help you camp. Handle's *Canoe Camping* is a stock favorite although not up-to-date with the freeze-dried foods. The American

Canoe Association offers *Canoe Cookery,* Part I & II at
10 cents each from ACA, 400 Eastern St., New Haven,
Conn. 06510. It contains much useful information, and
you can't beat the price.

Bradford Angier is a co-conspirator with the author
on attempting to lure people into the out-of-doors, and
his books go beyond camp cooking to cover wilderness
foods and survival. *Wilderness Cookery,* and *Free for
the Eating* are available anywhere, including STOW-A-
WAY PRODUCTS, for $3.95 and $4.95 respectively, and you
can't find better.

Maps

Every inch of the United States is mapped. You should
never head into any strange territory without a map
and/or chart of the waters and lands you will be roam-
ing. For all nautical charts, address United States Coast
& Geodetic Survey, Washington, D. C. 20013, or Canadian Hydrographic Service, Dept. of Energy, Mines &
Resources, Ottawa, Canada. Charts are generally $1.00.
Both departments offer guides to show you what charts
refer to which areas, but it has been my experience if
you describe carefully the area you want, they will send
it to you. Every state and Canadian Province is mapped
in detailed topographic maps that show all roads, trails,
elevations, streams, swamps and lakes, railroads and
what have you. Your local library can tell you where
to write for these. Maps of areas cost about 20 cents

apiece. Most of the United States has been mapped by aerial photography. For plains, mountain and Pacific states, address Western Laboratory, Aerial Photography Division, ASCS-USDA, 2505 Parley's Way, Salt Lake City, Utah 84109; for Mississippi, central, southern and eastern states, address Eastern Laboratory, Aerial Photography Division, ASCS-USDA, 45 South French Broad Avenue, Asheville, N. C. 28801. Maps cost about $1.50 for small scale, and huge (and expensive) enlargements are obtainable.

How to Get Started

Be forewarned that no one becomes an expert camper overnight. And it is the experts that the bugs don't bite, whose tents don't get washed away in midnight rain squalls and who remain cozy warm in cold snaps.

The way to start tent cruising is in your back yard or even on your living room floor. If you can't be comfortable there, you can be darn sure you'll be *miserable* in the boondocks. When you've mastered your tent, can make your stove bubble with happiness and your sleeping bag becomes an old pal, then you can step up. Try overnights near home. Stay close enough so you can get home if something goes wrong. Keep the trips short enough so you can pick favorable weather. When *that* campsite becomes an old friend—simple to get to, comfortable in all kinds of weather—and proves your equip-

ment reliable and complete, then take off for more ambitious projects.

I just bought some insurance from a man who is a
crack sailor. He is much in demand as he crews on ocean
racers and loves big boats. His own personal boat is a
Penquin. He just told me, "I like it because I'm not
married to it. I don't feel I have to use it."

Little boats are like that. So is this camping thing.
If you shelled out $4000 for a rugged truck camper,
you'd feel you must use it. With a $500 investment in a
sailing board or $100 worth of tent, it doesn't take much
fun out of it before the item is written off in your mind.
From there out, it's all pleasure. You can take it. Of
equal charm, you can leave it. You can play golf or watch
a ball game or read a book instead.

It's a nice feeling.

►VIII

Buying Used

Buying a used boat is like buying a used car. The most important thing as far as price is determined is whether or not the boat is "clean." Clean means new looking, not dirty, no scars, everything shiny bright.

Once, when selling boats, our firm had two 15½-foot sailboats side by side, one priced at $1600, the other at $1300. So help me the only difference was that someone had sailed the $1300 boat and scuffed and muddied the varnished floorboards. The very first time the $1600 boat was used, its floorboards would be scuffed the same way. The slight mar had nothing at all to do with the structure of the boat, its sail was in top condition, the fittings and wire were identical, but it possessed a "flaw" that saved some smart buyer a pile of money. It wasn't as clean.

What's involved is something we can recognize in ourselves. The complexities of modern automobiles are far beyond us all, including oftentime the mechanics charged with fixing them. If a used car looks good on the outside, in some strange way it gives us hope it will be okay on the inside.

Boats are no different. People have heard of all manner of dire and undiscoverable defects, and it worries them. If a boat looks like it has been well taken care of, it seems a reasonable conclusion it hasn't been neglected where it doesn't show.

Happily the advantages of little boats also extend to the used market. By virtue of their size they are easy to inspect, and aluminum and fiberglass construction is different from wood in that both are relatively free from hidden defects. Horrible things can happen internally where you can't see it in a wood boat. It is easy to build a punk boat out of either new material; but if the aluminum cracks, is torn or pops a rivet or two, there's no hiding it. Fiberglass, too, either cracks or doesn't crack. Even if someone tried to putty over cracks in a plastic boat he'd have to paint the whole boat inside and out to hide the defect. Fiberglass offers another plus in that it is scandleously easy to repair because layers of newly saturated cloth adhere perfectly to the old layers.

What you *don't* get buying used is model improvements. Not many people realize how hard it is to build a boat right the first time. In fact it is downright impossible. You can't gauge all the stresses. When the Sailfish first came out, their wood masts broke all the time. New masts of aluminum ended the problem. One small day sailor I know of lacked control on beam reaches. A new rudder shape corrected the condition. Look how outboard motors get lighter, less bulky and more economical year after year. I bought a fiberglass Blue Jay. The builder glued the deck supports to the side. The flexing tore them loose, and they had to be secured in place with fiberglass strips. The rest of the Blue Jays out of the builder's shop encorporated the improvement. One more bug hit the dust.

It's hard to put any time table on this de-bugging factor, but I hazard it takes at least three years before most of the errors have been found and corrected. If I were buying used, I'd be very cautious about the first few boats off a production line. This is more true in fiberglass where it is difficult to fully predict stress points. Sometimes the most minor modifications—more curve to an angle, a weight heavier cloth, another several bolts—can remedy big defects.

Depreciation

Any boat will lose between twenty and thirty-three per cent of its value the first year. This rate—roughly twenty per cent a year—will continue for two to three years until the boat is half depreciated. Here again the magic formula is "clean." If the boat is allowed to get shabby and neglected, expect the thirty-three per cent depreciation. If a boat stays bright and shiny, the lower rate will apply. After several years when the boat's value is roughly half of what it was new, condition rather than time becomes paramount. If you buy a three-year-old boat that lists for $1500 for $750, you can sell it three years later for $600 IF it is "clean."

In fact, you can reverse the trend. You can buy an abused boat several years old, clean it up with some elbow grease, paint and TLC and probably sell it for more money than you paid for it. I've done it many times.

Nor do you have to guess at what a boat is worth. Most everyone is aware of the "blue book" of automobile prices. This is a book that lists prices of every make and model of used car. If you ever had a car wrecked, you know about book value. It is what the insurance company will pay you for it—often to your dismay. The same service in several forms is available to boat dealers. BOATS UNLIMITED of Ft. Lauderdale, Fla., is the commonest on the east coast. If you are buying a used boat from a dealer and have reason to wonder about the price, ask to see the "blue book." If the dealer says he never heard of it or doesn't have such a book, smile knowingly and leave. He knows about it and subscribes to the service. If he doesn't, he won't be in business long.

What to Look For

Aluminum

Aluminum boats are either welded or riveted. Cracking along seams is common to both types of construction. These cracks may be hairline cracks, very hard to see. But if they are present, the boat will leak. Rivets loosen and sometimes pop out. Here, again, they show up by leaking. The structural members in aluminum boats— seat supports, transom knees, gunwales—are prone to breakage. Rivet leaks can be slowed by sealer gunked around the rivet, but best is to drill out the rivet and replace with a larger rivet. It is hard to locate a place that sells aluminum sheeting and rivets. If there is a boat builder near you, he'll sell them to you cheap. Otherwise an airport is your next best bet. They work in aluminum all the time, and it is much higher grade than boat aluminum. Aluminum can also be repaired by welding, but it is a very tricky material to work in. Only a few very professional welders will attempt it. Often keels and seams in aluminum boats are sealed by neoprene gasketing. In this case, they cannot be welded as the heat needed to fix one area would burn up the gasketing in another.

Probably rips and punctures are the most common damage to aluminum boats. These are relatively easy to deal with. The ripped area is flatted, sealer is spread over it, and a patch is riveted in place. I have seen alu-

minum canoes wrapped by raging rapids like a horse-
shoe around a rock. Incredibly they can be pounded
back into shape with rubber hammers and the long
cracks welded. I can assure you finding a welder capable
of doing this job won't be easy. (I can't find one in my
area.) Aluminum can also be patched with fiberglass
using epoxy resin. It is temporary, however. Sooner or
later the patch will come off.

The best book I know of on aluminum is *Aluminum
Boats* available at $2.00 from Kaiser Aluminum Sales,
Kaiser Center, Oakland, Cal. 95615.

Fiberglass

Fiberglass boats are made of a gel coat about as thick
as cigarette paper, then layers of glass saturated with
polyester resin. The glass cloth has a skeletal function,
just like reinforcing in cement. There are three kinds of
cloth, and you can tell something about a given boat by
seeing what kinds are used.

The strongest is roving. This shows a heavy, cross-
hatch pattern, almost like a basket weave. It is heavy
but rugged. Glass cloth is the commonest. It looks the
same as fiberglass curtains, the weave is neat and flat, and
it can be seen through the resin in the finished boat.
This cloth comes in a variety of thicknesses, however,
from four ounces per square yard to twenty ounces per
square yard. The heavier the cloth, the stronger the boat.
The weakest reinforcing is fiberglass mat. This is strands

of glass, pressed together. It creates an absolutely smooth surface.

Most fiberglass boats use combinations of the three reinforcing materials. Mat for the outside so the hull will be smooth, then two or three layers of roving or cloth depending on size and strength. I am comforted by the sight of roving in the interior of a hull because it suggests the builder has used the best available.

The first thing to deteriorate on a fiberglass boat is the gel coat. It will crack or fade. Waxing with regular car wax like Simonize will prolong its life. The surface can be buffed with a power buffer just like polishing an auto finish. If the gel coat is faded or cracked, the only remedy is filling all cracks with fiberglass putty, then painting with an epoxy paint. There are two kinds of fiberglass resins—polyester and epoxy. The latter is stronger and much more expensive. A polyester resin will stick well to itself if the surface has been washed with acetone. Epoxy is used as a glue and will stick to almost anything. It is widely used now in automobile body repair shops.

If a fiberglass boat has been punctured or cracked open, the technique for fixing it is to cut away the offending portions. Then the sides of the hole are ground down with wood rasp or circular power grinder and new layers of cloth laid one on top of the other until the hole is filled. Often waxed cardboard or plywood coated with cellophane, which the resin won't stick to, is used as a "form" to shape the glass until it "sets up"—

i.e., dries. This procedure is fairly simple if the break is not in a place where the shape is complicated. Even then a form can usually be fashioned out of such inexpensive stuff as newspaper dipped in flour a la kindergarten technique.

Old fiberglass boats can be painted. Usually the surface is roughed by sanding. New boats must be sanded and washed with acetone as wax is put in the mold to allow the boat to release. It clings to the hull for six months or so and will affect the adhesion of the new paint.

Buying a used fiberglass boat is usually a safe bet as after two or three years of service any defects will have appeared. Look the boat over carefully for cracks. Stress points around seats, transom, corners in the deck or hull or around the centerboard in a sailboat are vulnerable. While fiberglass is amazingly strong in impact and wear resistances, it does not hold fastenings well. Check that cleats and screws have not eroded their holes. I like to see them backed with wood. Much fiberglass construction utilizes a wood core, usually plywood, sandwiched in the plastic. In some cases this core has been known to rot. If panels compress in transom, stringers or floor, ask that a section of glass be cut out to inspect the wood section. It can be easily replaced. Fiberglass is not subject to corrosion, electrolysis, ice damage or rot. Any anti-fouling paint can be used with it.

Most of the wear and tear on plastic boats will be superficial. Correctly made boats are fantastically strong.

Recently I was examining a large fiberglass cruising sailboat that had been damaged in a storm. The bow was
abraded badly. Along one side you could see where
the boat had rubbed against a piling. In both places, the
gel coat was gone and you could see the layers of cloth
were eaten away. I was shaking my head when a man
walked by. "That's bad. But you should see the dock!"
I strolled out and could hardly believe my eyes. The
dock was ravaged! The bow of this boat had carved its
way through the two inch planking at least five feet. The
piling against which the boat had laid was almost worn
in two. A huge iron bolt had been bent and flattened
by the glass. Heavy supporting rails of the dock footing
were splintered. A wood boat would have been holed
and sunk six times over, and I'd estimate the big sloop
could have lasted hours longer before the timbers wore
their way through the hull and sank the boat.

An excellent book on fiberglass is readily available.
Fiberglass Boats, by Boughton Cobb, $2.50 from Yacht-
ing Books, 50 West 44th Street, New York, N.Y. 10036.

Used Outboard Motors

There isn't any question that the best place to buy
a used outboard motor is from a dealer who has recondi-
tioned it and offers you a warranty, usually ninety days.
You'll pay a higher price for such a motor, but the
service side of the outboard business is something of real
concern to all the bigger motor manufacturers. I've

watched factory-trained men tear engines down and when they put them back together, you've got a good deal. The warranty makes it an even better deal, especially if you make the motor work hard while uncovered headaches can be referred back to the dealer.

The next best way to buy a motor is to buy one you know runs well. Not just in a tank, but on a boat over a prolonged stretch. It is also wise to buy a used motor that hasn't been run hard, hot, under severe loads or a heck of a lot. How you determine this is all *caveat emptor*. All used motors have been owned by little old ladies and run gently and briefly only on sunny Sunday afternoons. The rate of motor depreciation is roughly the same as a boat. There is also a "blue book" on outboard prices.

Marine Surveyors

There are experienced persons who specialize in examining used boats in detail and giving a report of what they find. These surveys are extremely detailed. Long experience tells the surveyor where to look for trouble, and they seldom miss anything. Armed with their report of a boat's condition, you know exactly what problems you are, or are not, buying. They play an important part in price dickering. Cost for a survey of a large boat, a twenty-five-footer, for example, ranges in the $50 area, plus expenses: usually the cost of driving to and from the boat and meals. On any boat sizeable enough so that big money problems could result from an over-looked flaw, the survey cost is cheap insurance. In my opinion a buyer of any boat twenty-two feet or so ($3000 —up) is foolish not to have even a new boat surveyed. The chances are nine out of ten, the surveyor will turn up flaws, improper equipment (lights), incorrect, illegal or ill-advised installations, etc., which found before you buy, the dealer will fix to keep the sale. Afterwards, the dealer may or may not fix them depending on how badly he wants to retain your friendship.

On small boats where the cost may be in the $500—$600 area, the survey fee becomes a correspondingly larger bite. Most surveyors won't bother with small boats unless it is very convenient for them, and they aren't busy. The time needed to survey a small boat is obviously less than what would be required for a big vessel, but you will be amazed at the fine-tooth-comb approach they take even with a dinghy. By the time they are through they will have studied parts of the craft you didn't even realize were there, much less look at yourself. If you are very inexperienced or are getting into sizeable amounts of money, I strongly urge you seek the guidance of one of these experts. Buying a big boat without one calls to mind the legal adage that he who pleads his own case has a fool for a lawyer. He that surveys his own boat . . . etc. Most boatyards and all boat brokers and marine insurance agents can suggest surveyors in your area.

Sails

Sails are an important monetary consideration in the cost of most small day sailors. Cost of new sails ranges from about $75 for a Sailfish sail to twice that for more elaborate sails, especially if jib and spinnakers are involved. Dacron is what mainsails and jibs should be made of. Nylon is used for spinnakers. Mainsails and jibs made of any other material are virtually worthless and should be. Nylon quickly loses its shape, and cotton sails can be stretched out of shape by improper use and are short-lived even with the best of care. It is customary when buying a used sailboat to take the sails out of the bags and lay them out for close inspection. Look for tears and pin holes. The latter indicate age. Examine the stitching. Dacron cloth lasts a long time—ten years. But the stitching that holds the panels together does not sink in the fabric, but remains on top where it is subject to wear. If the Dacron is in good shape, a sailmaker can do wonders restoring an old sail and costs are very reasonable. ($15–$30 to completely resew a small sail.) Dacron sails should be washed with fresh water regularly and kept out of the sunlight as much as possible. Sails often become stained. This does no harm other than offending the eye. Cotton sails can be ruined by mildew which attacks the fibers. Dacron sails also mildew, but the fibers emerge unscatched although stains or discoloration will probably remain. Don't leave sails in a cold damp garage. Bundle in a cool dry place when not in

use. Also guard against mice. They love to chew up sails
to make nests. Lots of people try to make their own
sails, but few succeed. They are tricky to cut so as to
attain the essential airfoil shape that gives them power.
Rips, snags and holes, however, can be attended to by
the family seamstress. If you start serious racing, you
will soon start buying new sails frequently.

Summary

All in all, buying a good used small boat is a way to
pare costs roughly from one third to one half with little
risk, but probably a lot of looking. Newspaper classified
columns, boat yards and yacht clubs are good foraging
areas. Defects in the smaller boats are usually fairly
obvious. Except for some cartoppers or johnboats that
might be powered by oversized motors, little boats are
generally tougher in relation to the stresses on them than
big boats. This means they tend to last longer and are
thus attractive to second and third hand buyers. The
canoes and Sailfish-Sunfish probably retain the highest
resale value of the boats we have discussed. The less
known sailing boards, the catamarans and less popular
one-designs are probably about or above average. The
good neoprene inflatables even with a ten-year life probably depreciate most of all, and a rubber inflatable
would be a senseless buy after a couple of season's use.

IX

*Build It
Yourself*

There are a number of good reasons to build your own boat, but contrary to the hopes and expectations of thousands, economy is not always one of them. Even if you consider your time worthless (and all amateur boatbuilders do), you could sally forth any day and buy the same boat used for about what it will cost you to build.

The experience of many who have gone before you suggests that the *most* you can expect to save over the retail cost of the boat is two thirds. If a boat would sell at $3000, you can build it for $1000. However, this assumes a lack of certain unpleasantries we might as well face up to right now. If you make a mistake that requires rebuilding or rebuying, your cost goes up. You'll be buying quantities of lumber, fastenings, fiberglass, boat fittings, etc., which the boatbuilder buys at substantial discounts. To beat his cost, you've got to purchase at the same discount prices. Have you discount sources? You'll need a number of power tools and special tools. Ever see the number of clamps in a boatbuilder's shop? Hundreds! Is your tool investment already made? Since wood boat construction relies heavily on the use of glues, you'll have to build the boat in a temperature around seventy degrees. Do you have such a place or must you rent one or build one? Quite a number of large tasks even with small boats require two persons. Can you command free labor?

If you flunk out on any one of these, figure you'll be lucky to escape at less than fifty per cent of the retail cost. Then you must be prepared to face the reality that not all boats are sold at list price, more like ten per cent under. Now you are in the forty per cent bracket which is nice if it's your income tax rate, but a poor return on hours and hours of hard work. It must also be noted that hours of sheer agony are interspersed among the days of satisfaction at watching your special Venus rise from the lumber pile.

If I am being negative, it is deliberate. Building a dream boat, along with buying a thirty-year-old schooner and heading South, is a familiar pathway of broken dreams. How many boats have you seen that were instantly (and unfavorably) recognizable as "home-made"? When you figure that some poor Joe spent hours laboring, saved himself peanuts and wound up with an abortion, it simply doesn't make sense. He should have bought a good used boat.

Another negative growing in importance is that the amateur builder is restricted to wood. He can't build out of aluminum certainly and fiberglass probably not. Every day the popularity of wood boats diminishes. Yet not only must the amateur build in wood, if he has any sense he builds in plywood as it is the easiest. This restricts the shape of the boat. A really good trihederal hull, for example, like the Boston Whaler or a round-bottom boat, cannot be built out of plywood. The stuff won't bend enough.

On the other hand, for specialized boats like the west coast surf dory or duck boats, certain types of fishing boats and canoes, you almost have to build yourself. I've built a little duck boat every year for the last three years. I know just the kind of boat I need, and it isn't for sale. Also I can make it so simple and inexpensive that in the not-improbable event that a storm washes it away, I can shrug off the loss and build another.

Another advantage advanced by the home builder is that the method allows the cost of the boat to be spread over a long period of time. You dribble and drabble the money out. This is undeniable. But if you hold down a job today, you can get credit. And armed with this formidable commodity you can spread payments over five to seven years at almost any boat dealer via your friendly local banker (who will admittedly take a hunk of your hide in interest).

Boatbuilding the Smart Way

Having advanced all these reasonable attempts to discourage you, I now abandon the effort. After all, if you were a reasonable and intelligent person you wouldn't be reading this chapter anyway. Each man listens to a different drummer. If the tune beating into your ear is "get to the garage and build a boat," here are some new canny ways to go about it.

To understand the first way, you have to know something about professional boatbuilding. When a builder finishes a boat hull with cabin and decks, he figures only about twenty-five per cent of his work is done. Does that surprise you? It's true. Installing the engine (unless it is an outboard) requires another twenty-five per cent of his time and money. Building the interior—buying and installing head, sink and counter, stove and refrigerator, building bunks, dinettes, cabinets and such—is another quarter. Even after the whole boat is finished, the last twenty-five per cent of the time and money goes to painting the boat within and without. See why unpainted boats are so much cheaper?

If you get into cabin-sized boats built of fiberglass, a rough approximation will hold true. What pops out of the mold is a fractional part of the cost of the finished boat. Yet it is the most important part. It determines the boat's look. The materials and shape will determine the boat's strength. This shell of a fiberglass boat after deck and hull are properly joined is like the shell of an egg. Incredibly strong by design as well as material.

Although this shell represents but twenty-five per cent of the boat's cost, it is the crucial portion. If you are building in wood, the hull will take not require twenty-five per cent of your time, but more like fifty per cent. Nothing less than perfection is acceptable. Unless each underwater joint, for example, fits perfectly, the boat will leak. If a floor is not flush and true against the frame, its holding power is sapped. One frame mis-measured and the hull will be out of true.

It is when precision like this is demanded that the amateur falls down. Even plywood boats are curved where fitting one part to another is concerned. Almost none of the angles on boat parts are constant, but vary the length of the member. Making the elaborate, complex cuts can be done quickly and simply with the proper woodworking machines. To work it by hand with plane and saw requires hours of fitting and shaping. You'll see this factor when we cover kit boats. Almost all kit builders offer frame kits at surprisingly low cost. Their fancy shops can turn out members in minutes that it would take you or me hours to fashion. They know the smart amateur builder wants to put his time against the areas where he can make the most progress.

More and more home builders are using this principal with fiberglass boats. They buy what pops out of the mold and start building from there. One Maine firm offers thirty-four-foot hulls in the famous lobsterboat shape for $2800. To build that much hull yourself would take at least half that much money and a year of part-time labor. And you'd have a wood hull. Many cruising sailboat people offer hull, deck, cockpit assemblies. You finish off the interior.

Just because you start with fiberglass, doesn't mean you have to keep building with that material. Finish the hull and deck with wood. The interiors of big fiberglass boats are mostly wood anyway. I'm thinking of building a twenty-two-foot cabin garvey with stove, bunks, head, etc., so I can have a warm place to go when duck shooting. I'll buy a stock twenty-two-foot aluminum johnboat hull without seats, and bolt a $2'' \times 2''$ timber to the inside of the gunwale with stainless steel bolts. Then I'll build in plywood from this. Although more and more do, not all builders offer their boats in this unfinished form but I suspect an inquiry to most would produce a favorable reaction. After all, if they can price it to make a reasonable profit and sell direct without getting their dealer organization up in arms, why not?

Even in a small fiberglass sailor or runabout, much of the price of the boat grows out of the finishing. Installing decks, windshields, fitting cleats, motor cables, battery connections, lights and wiring, installing the steering, are all part of a score of odd jobs that take time. If you'd visited as many fiberglass boat plants as I have, you could close your eyes and see workers polishing by the hour with elaborate buffers and grinding compounds all for one purpose—a mirror finish. Make the mirror finish yourself (or forget it) and you incorporate the best of all worlds. You have a modern boat, made from modern materials. But you have saved yourself roughly half.

Kit Boats

The complexities of wood-boat construction vary greatly. Toughest to build are probably round-bottom, carvel-planked boats, because frames (ribs) must be steam-bent in elaborate forms. Next in complexity is lap-strake planking where the planks overlap one another. Each must be fitted with exacting deliberation. Strip planking is an easier construction as small planks are edge-nailed to one another, and the boat is formed around a few molds as is the case in lap-straked boats. Framing and/or support is installed later. Today a strip-built boat would be built light, extensively glued, and heavily fiberglassed.

Plywood construction is the easiest of all. Even elaborate plywood designs use mostly straight lines as the material can be bent in only one direction, and reluctantly at that. However, certain plywood types are easier than others. One in particular, the Texas dory, has a flat bottom, and you can readily see building a flat bottom-boat is easier than installing a "V" in the bottom.

You can find boat-building plans in various magazines

from time to time. But there's no question in my mind
that this is a bad place to look for them. I've had a hand
in several of these publications, and the trouble with
them is the designs have not usually been built by the
man who designed them. They may be easy enough to
build if the designer knows what he's doing, but often
they are poorly planned. Some come off the drawing
board of mail-order design school architects and are
more in the order of pipe-dreaming on paper than anything. I'm not against pipe dreaming. But don't let
somebody else's pipe dream turn out to be your head-
ache because the illustration, the "artist's conception,"
of the final boat looked great. Also the first-boat-bugs
principal very much applies to these designs.

There are a surprising number of firms that specialize
in plans for the boat builder. You can be assured that
these designs have been built, they are time-tested. I
know some of the men who run these outfits, and another invaluable service they perform is advice. If you
start building and get stuck, you can write them a letter
and they'll help you.

Another short cut they offer is pre-cut and pre-lofted
plans. When you start to build a boat, you have to "loft
it," that is, draw the boat, full-size on huge pieces of
paper or cheap plywood. It is a tedious but necessary
task, because the designers make so many mistakes in
their figures—among other things. It is like making a
pattern the way dressmakers do. You can see that if you
have a curved stem to cut, drawing it from a pattern

would be a heck of a lot easier than measuring and fairing (i.e., making smooth) the gradual and complex curves.

Besides offering patterns at slight extra expense over the plans alone, the kit builders also offer frame kits. This carries the process one step further. The companies cut and often pre-assemble the vital parts of the boat.

Here are some sample prices:

12-foot Catamaran: Plans only $10; Plans & Pattern, $20; Building kit, $110.

17-foot Outboard Cruiser with two-bunk cabin; Plans, $10; Plans & Patterns, $16.75; Frame kit, $115.

25-foot Inboard Cruiser: Plans, $20; Plans & Pattern, $35; Cabin Patterns, $20; Frame set, $350.

Freight in all cases is extra and would add another $25—$75.

Kit builders advertise in the outdoor and how-to-do-it magazines. Here's a list of all I can find.

GLEN L. MARINE, 9152 Rosecrans, Bellflower, Cal. 90706. Catalogue 50 cents. Contains about eighty boats, some helpful information. I know the owner of this small but progressive company and suggest anyone interested in the subject study his catalogue before proceeding further.

CLEVELAND BOAT BLUEPRINT CO., Box 18250, Cleveland, Ohio 44118. Catalogue 60 cents. Inboard, outboard, sailboats from 7½—33 ft.

CLARK CRAFT, 16-X Aqua Lane, Tonawadin, N. Y.,

14150. Catalogue $2.00 (world's largest they claim), 250 designs.

MOTOR BOATING, 959 8th Avenue, New York, N. Y. 10019. Free catalogue of boat plans. No patterns or kits here but lots of traditional-type boats.

LUGER, 9200 Bloomington Freeway, Bloomington, Minn. 55431. Free catalogue. Includes fiberglass shells. Boat 12–32 ft.

One of the most famous flat-bottom boats ever built is the Grand Banks dory. These seaworthy vessels need no introduction, and the fact that their design is simple and cheap to build (which is why the fishermen used them in the first place) is no less important today—especially to the boatbuilder. There is a company that specializes in adapting the basic dory to various sizes and shapes including sailing versions. Most people don't realize what a splendid craft this is. Send $1.00 to TEXAS DORY BOAT PLANS, Box 720, Galveston, Texas 77551, and study the package, and you'll find out.

Canoe Kits

There are a number of builders offering both wood and fiberglass canoes and kayaks in plan or kit form. First among them is my friend Mr. Bruce Clark, 115 McGavock Pike, Nashville, Tenn. 37214. He offers a free catalogue that describes the many designs he offers. In addition, look to these sources for canoes you can build.

KAYAK KIT, Box 582, Willoughby, Ohio 44094. Free literature.

SPORTSCRAFT, Box 8393, Columbus, Ohio 43201. Canoes and kayaks, kits and plans, many styles and lengths. Free literature.

RIVERSIDE CANOES, Box 5595, Riverside, Cal. 92502. Four fiberglass canoe kits. Free literature.

TRAILCRAFT, Box 33, Glasco, Kansas 67445. Five models of fiberglass and wood and canvas canoe kits. This is probably the biggest plastic canoe kit concern. I built one of these canoes and found it very easy to put together.

Books and Literature

There are plenty of books offering helpful advice to the prospective (or immersed!) boatbuilder.

Boatbuilding by H. I. Chapelle is the granddaddy of them all. It covers all kinds of classic construction and, although written pre-fiberglass, reads easier than most. I've spent many a happy hour over this grand work, and the author's confident yet light approach to the subject adds zest to the vast encompass of knowledge contained therein. Chapelle constantly refers to the "groaning chair" with which every boatbuilder must equip his shop. When you goof, you go sit in the chair and groan.

GLEN L. MARINE offers three books written by the owner. *Boatbuilding with Plywood,* $7.50. *Inboard Motor Installation in Small Boats,* $6.00. *How to Build Boat Trailers,* $3.00.

Fiberglass Boats You Can Build and *Workable Plans for Practical Boats,* both available from Motor Boating. Ask for free full list of their books at the same time.

DOUGLAS FIR PLYWOOD ASSO., 119 A. Street, Tacoma, Wash. 98402, offers a well-written twelve-page pamphlet, *Plywood & Kits,* 25 cents.

As you will quickly find when you start a purchasing campaign, chi chi boat lamps at fancy prices are easy to find. Finding a wide selection of equipment, suitable fastenings, many hull and deck fittings at any price, much less discount prices, is extremely difficult. Fortunately there are a number of mail order concerns that will sell at realistic prices and whose inventories are copious.

JAMES BLISS AND CO., 100 Route 128, Dedham, Mass. 02026, and MANHATTAN MARINE, 116 Chambers Street, New York, N. Y. 10007, both sell their giant catalogues for $1.00 and will enclose with the least excuse a discount sheet. They carry boat equipment of all kinds, but their main emphasis is on hardware. Tanks, hoses, fittings, fastenings, chairs, horns, goosenecks, ropes, winches—you name it, they've got it.

Two relatively new mail order boat retailers are aggressively discounting both boat hardware and accessory equipment—mops, compasses, radios, Radio Direction Finders, chairs, seats, rope, everything but the basic nuts and bolts. Prices are discounted in the catalogues of each. GOLDBERGS, 202 Market Street, Philadelphia, Pa. 19106, offers their catalogue for $1.00. DEFENDER IN-

DUSTRIES, 384 Broadway, New York, N. Y. 10013, offers theirs for 50 cents. DEFENDER has the widest selection of fiberglass materials, including Dynel and Vectra fibers, and much useful information on the selection and use of all fiberglass. All the foregoing carry items for sailboats—wire, winches, turnbuckles and the like. However, if you are building a sailing vessel, MERRIMAN BROS., 100 Industrial Park Road, Hingham, Mass. 02043, and WILCOX-CRITTENDEN, Middletown, Conn. 06457, are two venerable firms that dominate the sailboat fittings field. Both catalogues are $1.00, and neither firm, to my knowledge, is given to casual discounting. Alas.

If you plan to build a wood boat of any size, you should know all about fastenings. The H. M. HARPER CO., Morton Grove, Ill. 60053, in their *Fastener Guide to and for the Marine Industry* and magnificent *Harper Handbook* offer the best guide and the most assortment of materials from stainless through aluminum and even nylon and titanium. If MANHATTAN MARINE or BLISS can't furnish what fastenings you need, address HARPER. If they can't furnish it, abandon the project.

Organization

It used to be that anyone building a boat was pretty much on his own. Now he can have friends-in-need in the form of Jim Betts and his buddies. Betts, a former White Plains' public relations man, has founded the International Amateur Boat Building Society with offices

at 111 Woodcrest Avenue, White Plains, N. Y. 10604.
Already the group boasts some three thousand members
in fourteen chapters in this country and Canada. In
Chicago, Detroit, Oklahoma City, and Boston, members
have solved the always formidable problem of finding
building space by renting lofts where as many as two
dozen boats are building at any one time. By a quarterly
publication amateur builders are kept abreast of each
other's triumphs and tragedies (tragedies outnumber triumphs by three to one, says Betts). Members also enjoy
extreme discount rates by concentrating purchasing
power. Most of all, what this needed organization can
offer you is good advice: Take stock; think small; use
tested plans; and don't undertake projects that will require more than three years' building time are basic
tenets.

There is no better testimony to the difficulties of
building a substantial boat yourself than these eloquent
words that appeared recently in *Yachting* magazine. At
the launching of his completed ship, one young builder
wrote: "I made a vow never to build another boat. I
was tied, thin, rundown and almost broke. I had lost
contact with friends and things around me while giving
my entire efforts to the wood and metal thing that floated
so gingerly on the water. But someone once said that
nothing of any value or beauty came into this world
without labor or pain. I believe this for I have *Hum-
ming Bird* to prove it."

Renting

I have a thirty-two-foot Dickerson ketch named the *Lady Mary*. She's a roomy old plug of a boat, slow but comfortable. I keep her down on Maryland's lower Choptank, and every spring I take off and cruise for a week in the enchanting rivers and islands of Chesapeake Bay. We anchor out every night and sleep with the music of the wind in the rigging and the slap of the waves against the bow.

The most remarkable thing about this boat is that someone else takes care of it for me. Another man pays the yard bills, worries it through storms, fixes things, scrapes and paints, buys new equipment, arranges for the insurance and performs a host of similar tasks, large and small. You can see how good a deal it is for me when I tell you this fellow has over $8000 invested in the boat while I have over $8000 invested in General Motors stock. This makes sense to me because over the years I have watched the value of the *Lady Mary* steadily decline, while the value of General Motors stock has increased with equal inevitability.

Of course, this fellow owns *Lady Mary* all the time, while I only own the boat for that week. But a week is all I want to own it. And if you think about the boats like *Lady Mary* you see empty and wasted, weekend after weekend, you can see why. Big boats owned by busy men often aren't used more than several weeks a year. Yet they have no one to pay the yard bills, worry them through storms, fix things, etc., as I do.

Chartering like I do can give the very best in boating. You have all the fun, all the excitement and thrills of big boat sailing and cruising. Yet at the end of the cruise all the worries, expenses, broken things, scratches, varnished spots, etc., are turned over to another. You step ashore and let him fix them. It's a grand feeling, let me tell you.

Renting a boat, chartering is just a fancy name for it, isn't very popular. I'm inclined to feel the reason is intimidation. People hold the big boats in awe. Certainly the price is reasonable enough. The *Lady Mary* costs me $50 a day, which is split in half as my wife and I cruise with another couple. Expenditure of $150 for six days' lodging is peanuts. It would cost half that to stay in a motel. Being able to do your own cooking saves you a bundle. Bigger boats that can carry three couples with ease charter in the $75–$100 a day range. The same sort of economy prevails.

Since this is so, and since here is yet another way to enjoy the pleasures and visit the haunts of millionaire boaters, it most certainly should be included in a book devoted to economical boating. After all, we aren't restricted to little boats, just little expenditure. Sneaky tip: When you sail up in your gorgeous yacht and the people on the dock ooo and ah, you don't have to tell them you don't pay the bills on it, worry it through storms, fix things, etc. Just smile.

There are two general kinds of charter arrangements. The first is where you hire a boat with a professional captain to run it. He is under your orders and goes when and where you want, excepting only if he feels conditions don't warrant it. Usually this kind of arrangement applies to big boats, fifty feet and up, where you'd be lucky to get the boat for a few days for our magic $1000 dollar figure.

The poor man's version of this kind of professional captaincy are the various cruise ships that ply the Maine coast, the Virgin and Bahama Islands and elsewhere. Here you join a dozen or so strangers on a pre-planned cruise. The ship's company runs the vessel. These cruises are great. You see wonderful waters. Usually the ships are character vessels, fun to be on and help sail. Any travel agent can give you a list of them. Costs vary, but they aren't expensive—$200 a week including all food for one.

Obviously there is more satisfaction in handling the boat yourself, if you can. You do exactly what you please with it. This is called bareboat chartering. The boat is "bare" of any crew, but fully equipped. You bring linens (sleeping bags are best) and food and soothing liquids.

Boating magazines carry ads by owners offering their vessels for bareboat charters. Prices average between $350–$500 a week depending on size and elegance of the vessel. Another area to seek boats for charter is through boat brokers. Often skippers who have listed their boats for sale will consider a charter to help meet the expenses. The biggest bareboat (and cruise ship) area today is astonishingly enough in the Virgin Islands. Here invariably superb weather, little tide or fog, and sunny island-hopping itineraries create near-perfect boating conditions. Near perfect? Conditions are perfect. The charter boats (mostly sailboats) don't cost any more, booze is cheap, the girls prettier, the fishing great, and everywhere you look delights the eye. Alec Waugh said that, but a native put it this way to me: "Climb de hill, and your eyes will take pleasure." I climbed the hill, and I can still close my eyes and take pleasure.

Millionaire stuff to think about a charter in those breath-taking islands? Not a bit of it. One Virgin Island bareboat charter company equips the boats with all necessary food, booze, ice, fuel, outboard-equipped dinghy, beer and soft drinks. Cost of boat so-loaded $700 per week for a thirty-foot boat sleeping five adults comfortably. If you go with another couple, you're in for

$350 apiece. Plane fare to St. Thomas is $240 for two. You don't have to spend any nights ashore. At the most your extra cost would be taxi rides, gift buying and eating in the superb little restaurants that are cropping up around many of the common anchorages. It may be living like a millionaire, that I'll admit. But it doesn't cost like it. WARNING: be prepared if you take this trip to come back with island fever. There is no known cure. Long Island Sound, Florida Coasts—east and west, the coast of Maine and the Chesapeake around Annapolis are other prime charter and cruising areas.

Houseboats

The new cruising houseboats that have become so popular are giving rise to a new boating phenomena: houseboat rental agencies. These are located along most of the more famous waterways, in larger impoundments and lakes, on the more sheltered sounds and bays. Most rental agencies use boats in the thirty to forty foot range, and prices will be comparable to chartering other boats of equal value. Figure prices from $250 to $450 a week, food and fuel not included, but all necessary gear except linen provided.

There are two good sources to locate houseboat rental agencies. RENT-A-CRUISE OF AMERICA has seventy-five franchised agencies throughout the country. Address them at Box 781, Florence, Ala. 35630. The INTERNATIONAL HOUSEBOAT ASSOCIATION, Box 610, Jeffersonville,

Ind. 47130, maintains a current listing of rental agencies which is free upon request. *Family Houseboating* offers what is probably the most complete listing. It can be had for 50 cents from Family Houseboating, Box 2081, Tolluca Lake, Cal. 91602.

Canoe Rentals

The lack of a canoe need not deter you from the fun of cruising in one. Ely, Minnesota, is the canoe capital of the world (so they claim), and any number of outfitters there will rent you the gear you need to set forth into the Quetico-Superior National Park and the newly established boundary waters between the United States and Canada. Cost for these rentals is within the reach of anyone. The basic rental price is $8 a day, which furnishes food, canoe, sleeping bags, cooking gear, tent, etc., for two. All you need bring are personal items, clothes and the bag of bones you inhabit. Here is a partial list of outfitters. A note to any will bring further details.

WILDERNESS OUTFITTERS, Box 29, Ely, Minn. 55731.

QUETICO-SUPERIOR CANOE OUTFITTERS, Box 787, Ely, Minn. 55731.

BILL ROM CANOE COUNTRY OUTFITTER, 626 East Sheridan Street, Ely, Minn. 55731.

BORDER LAKE OUTFITTING, Box 569, Ely, Minn. 55731.

GUNFLINT NORTHWOODS OUTFITTERS, Box 5, Grand Marais, Minn. 55604.

PIPESTONE OUTFITTING, Box 780, Ely, Minn. 55731.

The famous Allagash River in Maine has at least one large canoe cruise outfitter. Address: ALLAGASH WILDERNESS OUTFITTERS, Star Route 22236, Greenville, Me. 04441.

Boat Liveries

Boating at its barest minimum is hiring a boat—usually a johnboat or flat-bottom rowboat at a livery for a day or half day. It is generally the least satisfactory way to get afloat. The boats are usually nondescript tubs to begin with, poorly maintained and unsafe. Motors are uncertain. If you hire boats from this kind of place, insist on oars, good life preservers and a good anchor. And if you plan to do it on any kind of regular basis, read this book. You can own your own boat and save money.